Bluebird
a dream of a boat

COLLECTORS' BOOKS LIMITED

Maurice Maeterlinck (1862-1949) after whose play The Blue Bird, *all Malcolm Campbell's boats and cars were named, the inspiration for the name* Blue Bird

Bluebird

**a dream of a boat
in six Acts**
(after Maeterlinck)

by

Martin Summers

Illustrated by Scott Beadle

COLLECTORS' BOOKS LIMITED

First published in Great Britain, 1990
by Collectors' Books Limited,
Bradley Lodge, Kemble, Cirencester
Gloucestershire GL7 6AD
© Martin Summers, 1990

Printed in Great Britain by Jolly & Barber

Design by Christian Brann

Research by Mark Child

Illustrations by Scott Beadle

ISBN 0 946604 03 7

Blue Bird, *Sir Malcolm Campbell's first
commissioned boat, on the Thames in 1931*

Foreword

Since the Association of Dunkirk Little Ships was formed, the long arm of coincidence, the finger of fate or the Hand of Divine Providence (according to how you feel about such things) have been a constant influence in its affairs. This is not surprising, since each ship in the Association has her own astonishing story. Some are well publicised; others effectively unknown. But having participated in one of the most remarkable events in the entire history of warfare, it is impossible that this should not be so.

During 'Operation Dynamo' itself, what may well be considered "matters of chance" repeatedly influenced the course of history - nine days of extraordinarily calm seas for a start.

Thus in this account of the origins of one of those Little Ships and what subsequently befell her, we read a tale typical in many respects, but at the same time unique to *Bluebird of Chelsea*. Clearly she has been a lucky ship, not least in her current ownership. Had she not been rescued from almost certain extinction by a man of meticulous taste, she would not enjoy her present splendour. Had he not had the wherewithal, as well as the inclination, to lavish a small fortune on her, she could well have emerged as a mere shadow of her former self. Had he not been a man of easy charm and generous spirit, she would not have become, so comparatively quickly, a popular sister in the exclusive company of her siblings.

And finally, thanks to the manner in which she is skippered and crewed, she is by no means a pretty toy, but a serious sea-going yacht which continues to log a cruising record capable of rousing the envy of many a hardened "blue water man". So, *Bluebird of Chelsea* has been a lucky ship. But she is also a happy ship. Long may she continue to be both.

Raymond Baxter,
Hon. Admiral, Association of Dunkirk Little Ships

5

Martin Summers, the owner of Blue Bird since 1984, who restored her and renamed her Bluebird of Chelsea *with his daughter Tara*

6

Prologue

Boats, especially traditional wooden ones, get a hold on you, more than any other possessions. This is how it was with me when I became involved with *Bluebird of Chelsea*. You feel compelled to cherish such a boat, spend your time and all your resources on her and think about her, day and night.

In return you reap undreamed-of pleasure and access to a whole new world. *Bluebird of Chelsea* has brought me into close personal contact with war heroes, Thames watermen, sailors, students of ships and history. I have come to see the world from an entirely new viewpoint, so that it will never be quite the same again for me. Hampton Court, the Tower of London and the Houses of Parliament seen from the River Thames take on a timeless and romantic aspect. At the wheel of your own ship you can relate to Samuel Pepys, Henry VIII, Sir Thomas Moore - all of whom used this ancient highway, which has hardly changed since their day. I was also introduced to Maurice Maeterlinck whose play *The Blue Bird* gave my ship her name. From her mooring at Cadogan Pier in Chelsea she has taken us through the inland waterways of Holland and France and as far afield as the Western Isles of Scotland.

Without Scott Beadle none of this would have been possible. His nautical knowledge, his Yorkshire humour and the range of his talents never cease to amaze me. With Scott and Graham Parker, I am fortunate to have such a fine team. This book is a tribute to the legend of the blue bird of happiness, to Sir Malcolm Campbell, for whom *Blue Bird* was built, and to the brave crew who 50 years ago sailed *Blue Bird* to the rescue of our troops at Dunkirk. I also want to pay tribute to all those who helped me to restore *Bluebird of Chelsea* with the skill and care which will enable her to continue as a proud member of the Association of Dunkirk Little Ships for many years to come.

" . . . Listen to me! . . . All of us here present, Animals, Things and Elements, possess a soul which man does not yet know. That is why we retain a remnant of independence; but if he finds the Blue Bird, he will know all . . . "
Maeterlinck, *The Blue Bird.*

7

Prologue

Finally, I would like to thank Christian Brann and his team at Collectors' Books, for their help and encouragement in producing this book. In particular Mark Child, whose research has been exhaustive. It was he who tracked down previous owners and unearthed such a treasure trove of fascinating anecdotes and details. The quality of all Christian Brann's publications speaks for itself. He is one of those people who can take an idea and turn it into a reality with the minimum of fuss. Without his guidance and support, we would have fallen into many of the inevitable pitfalls associated with this type of project.

Blue Bird is now nearly sixty years old and has never looked better. Many, many people have contributed to her present well-being and she can now face the future with confidence. *Bluebird of Chelsea* is indeed a happy ship.

Martin Summers,
Chelsea, June 1990

Sir Malcolm Campbell on board the newly completed **Blue Bird** *in 1931*

8

ACT ONE

The Dream Begins

" . . . I can do without the grass that sings, at a pinch; but I must absolutely have the Blue Bird. It's for my little girl . . . she wants to be happy . . ."

Maeterlinck, *The Blue Bird*

Malcolm Campbell as a young man, when he was influenced by Maeterlinck's play

It was a Sunday afternoon in late November 1984 when it all started. My four-year-old daughter Tara and I were strolling along Chelsea Embankment with some friends, admiring the boats moored at Cadogan Pier by Albert Bridge. The lights on the bridge had just come on, there was a spectacular sunset and I was thinking how beautiful it all was with the boats bobbing around on their moorings, as if trying to keep warm. Suddenly with the spontaneity typical of a four year old, Tara asked, "Daddy, why don't *we* have a boat"?

That simple question, to which I had no good answer, provoked a chain of events which sees me now, six years later, attempting to write the history of a famous boat and how I became her proud owner. For someone who knew precious little about boats, this was a major undertaking. I was 46 years old, an art dealer living in Chelsea, with the Thames almost lapping at my doorstep. Though I am knowledgeable about impressionist paintings, I knew nothing about boats. But that wasn't really a good enough answer. After all, I knew nothing about impressionist paintings until I applied myself to the subject.

So I took the idea to Scott Beadle, who has a great deal of experience of boats. To cut a long story short, within a week he had found me one which has given me more pleasure than I could ever have imagined. But even Scott, when he said "Leave it to me", could not have known that he would find a boat associated with one of the most famous Englishmen of the 20th century, a boat which had survived the greatest rescue operation of World War II, with a history full of dramatic events and colourful characters. Originally

Albert Bridge, with Cadogan Pier beside it. This is where it all began

11

The statue of Eros in the centre of Piccadilly Circus, the heart of London's Theatreland

Blue Bird, or *Bluebird of Chelsea* as she is now, was commissioned by Sir Malcolm Campbell in 1931, but the story of how and why he was to call all his cars and boats by that name starts many years before.

For the beginning, we have to go back to the Edwardian London of 1909. In the West End the smash hit of the year, *Our Miss Gibbs* with Gertie Millar and George Grossmith, was halfway through its run at the Gaiety Theatre. *The Arcadians* was on at the Lyric, and Lily Elsie and Joe Coyne had turned a speculative venture into a huge success with *The Dollar Princess*. The London stage, late in 1909, was dominated by these three productions. During the period of the Christmas holidays, the popular alternative to the musical at the time was the fairy play, with its appeal to both children and adults. *Fallen Fairies* by W. S. Gilbert and Edward German opened to good reviews at the Savoy, and *Where Children Rule* provided a fantasy kingdom for the young at the Garrick. As the year drew to a close, Olive Walter and Pauline Gilmer were preparing to open at the Haymarket in another fairy play, but one which was to be the best received of all. The famous Belgian playwright Maurice Maeterlinck's *L'Oiseau Bleu* came to the London stage not, as usual, fresh from a premiere in Paris, but via Constantin Stanislavski's production in Moscow.

The first-night audience would have come mostly in horse-drawn cabs with the ladies bedecked in dresses possibly from the newly opened Selfridges, and maybe sporting the year's hairdressing sensation, the first 'permanent wave'. There were few cars on the streets in those days, all of them restricted under the Motor Cars Act of 1903 to 20 m.p.h. In view of the effect the play was to have on Campbell, one of the fastest men of his time, this was indeed ironic. The effect it had on the critics was unprecedented. *The Times* described the play as "an evening

12

of unalloyed happiness", and "an exquisite blend of fancy, wisdom, speculation, poetry, tenderness, and pure beauty". *The Stage* called it "delicate and imaginative stage art", and observed that "the reception last night by a crowded and distinguished audience was enthusiastic". The cast performed another of Maeterlinck's fantasies of life, death and the pursuit of the unobtainable, plunging themselves through the full range of theatrical emotions. Few of the audience, the critics felt, would not be moved by the experience.

The elusive bluebird is an enduring character from mythology kept alive by folklore and fairy tale. Maeterlinck acknowledged his own source to be provincial French legend from Lorraine, but it is part of the bluebird folklore that efforts to locate this in the area have failed, suggesting that the bluebird of happiness was in fact a product of Maeterlinck's own imagination. For Capt. Malcolm Campbell, the play *The Blue Bird* was to be an experience he would never allow himself to forget, and he has made the name synonymous with British craftsmanship, a sense of adventure and achievement.

Theatre Royal, Haymarket, London, where Maeterlinck's **Blue Bird** *was first performed in England*

Whether or not Campbell actually went to the opening night is difficult to establish. Probably he went early in 1910, when he was 25 years old, on the advice of a friend. By this time Campbell was already involved with motor racing and had called two of his cars *Flapper I* and *Flapper II* after a not particularly distinguished race horse. He had just bought the 1909 Vanderbilt Cup-winning car, a Darracq, and was about to name it *Flapper III*, but something he heard in the play inspired him to change his mind. He kept his theatre programme, which now belongs to Kevin Desmond, the historian who has written extensively about Campbell and possesses over twenty different editions of Maeterlinck's play translated into several languages.

13

Campbell's third Darracq was to be his first motor vehicle named Blue Bird

During the performance, Campbell made an impulsive decision. As soon as the curtain came down he rushed back to his home in Bromley and, regardless of the lateness of the hour, woke up a neighbour who owned a car body paintshop. Having selected the right blue, he then spent the rest of the night and the early hours of the morning painting the Darracq. Shortly after dawn, still in his paint-splattered overalls, he drove straight to Brooklands and proceeded to win two races that day. This clear vindication of his rash decision, coupled with the car's subsequent good performances, ensured that the name would last through three superstitious generations of speeding Campbells. Long after the final curtain had fallen on Maeterlinck's play, long after the book went out of print, his idea of a fabled bluebird of happiness remains part of our language.

The name appeared on a whole succession of reincarnations: racing cars, motor yachts and power boats, and even his plane, each one the tangible factor in Campbell's pursuit of something unobtainable. For every speed record set was only there to be bettered, either by Campbell or his competitors. And the early stage which he and Henry Segrave had to themselves, soon saw a clutch of hopefuls stepping out of the wings.

Just before he died, Campbell's long-time mechanic Leo Villa wrote in his book, *Life With The Speed King*, "I was soon to learn that Campbell was an exacting type of person who considered that nothing was impossible". The name *Blue Bird* was, in effect, a constant reminder of what he hoped to achieve for himself.

Brooklands, racing cars and speed were to become the most important aspects of his life from then on, combined with an uncanny knack for making money as an insurance underwriter. His involvement with boats seems to have started as early as 1908, with a cruise up the Thames in a small river launch. Campbell once reminisced to Leo, "Ah they were good times, Villa, 1908 - wine, crumpet, songs, quiet cruising up and down the Thames - nothing to beat it. I'd give my eye teeth to have them back again". No further record of cruises exist until 1926 when he made an amazing voyage seeking buried treasure. This lure of hidden riches absorbed him throughout his life, and later in 1939 aged 54, he was to build a boat specifically to hunt for treasure in the South Seas. But in 1926, he joined Lee Guinness in his converted Liverpool pilot boat *Adventuress* on a voyage to Cocos Island, in the Pacific, west of Columbia, isolated and reputedly uninhabited. It was said to contain hoards of pirate treasure which had lain undiscovered for centuries: the plundered wealth of the 17th century brigand Edward Davies, that of the scurrilous Benito Bonito and - most

Adventuress, *Lee Guinness' yacht photographed in 1925*

15

desirable of all - the great riches of Lima Cathedral. But the island was to keep its mysteries, and remain a place of myth and legend, bloodshed and expeditions doomed to failure.

The *Adventuress* was an ocean-going yacht which undoubtedly fired Campbell's imagination, and may well have been a mental blueprint for his own later vessels. She survived everything which nature threw at her during the voyage, as did the crew, who were sustained by thoughts of what they might accomplish. No more successful in raising the great riches of Lima than its forerunners, the Campbell/ Guinness expedition came home after two weeks, leaving Malcolm to spend the rest of his life in the hope of going back properly organised and with some invention that would take the uncertainty out of treasure hunting. This expedition may well have been the latent catalyst for his own succession of motor yachts. Here was Campbell the acquisitor perhaps now genuinely impressed by life on board, and Campbell the headstrong who, after all, had tried to own most other forms of transport including an aeroplane. However he justified it one will never know, but before the 1930s Malcolm Campbell was toying with the idea of buying a motor boat.

This first craft was nowhere near as ambitious as its successors. In 1929 Campbell suddenly announced to Leo Villa that he had bought a boat, and it was quite clear to the mechanic that his expertise was going to be taken as much for granted in this new enterprise as it was in the others. Villa, nearly 15 years younger than his master, was an Italian cockney who had by then been with Campbell for about six years. He knew nothing about boats except that his paternal grandfather had been the captain of a paddle steamer in Switzerland. He once wrote, "Up to that time my only connection with boats had either been on a paddle steamer with my family, or possibly in a rowing boat on the

16

Serpentine in Hyde Park". Clearly if Malcolm wished to derive his fun from experiencing the unknown, Leo Villa was to do likewise.

The boat which Campbell had so precipitously bought was a small 34' Thornycroft cabin cruiser, already a few years old, called *Billduan*, probably similar to the craft he had cruised on the Thames many years earlier. She was powered by two twin-cylinder Handy Billy petrol engines and had twin propellers. On 2nd August Campbell, Leo Villa and Col. Colin Defries, a friend of the owner, set forth from Hampton Wick on the first voyage bound for the South Coast. Calling at Cadogan Pier they picked up an untried, self-professed Thames expert called Swift, who was to act as pilot, but by the time they got to Ramsgate they had fallen out and Swift was replaced by one Charlie Knight.

Billduan, *Campbell's cabin cruiser, which became the first of his yachts called* Blue Bird

The weather had no respect for the novice owner and his crew and *Billduan*, as she was still called, pitched so violently in the big seas that the crockery was smashed, the gramophone was thrown to the floor and Campbell himself was knocked unconscious. They persevered, however, and eventually arrived at Bosham in Sussex, where he intended to keep the boat. Soon she was rechristened *Blue Bird*, but except on rare occasions, his wife Dolly refused to share his enthusiasm for this new sport. Although he was a skilled driver of cars, Campbell seemed to have experienced certain difficulties adjusting to the 'helm', and there are many stories of embarrassing situations, the least of them going aground. Leo Villa was not a born sailor either but stoically acted as crew on the regular trips Campbell liked to make. The high point of the year was when the whole family and crew went to watch the Schneider Cup race in perfect conditions. So, in late September she was on her way back, once again in choppy seas in the Thames Estuary bound for Hampton Wick for a refit. This time the journey took nearly three hours longer.

Campbell was still racing but was concentrating more and more on the world land speed record. 1931 was to be a momentous year for him. On 5th February at Daytona Beach, he pushed the record to a fantastic 246.09 m.p.h. In recognition of this feat and previous successful efforts, on 19th February on his return to Britain from the U.S.A., he received a Knighthood. Sadly the reception committee for Campbell and his record breaking *Napier-Campbell Bluebird* had to go home and the celebrations were delayed as the *Mauretania*, on which he had travelled with Charlie Chaplin and Steve Donoghue, was many hours late, having run aground on the West Brambles on entering the Solent. It was only at 10.15 p.m. that he stepped ashore at Southampton and read, apparently by the light of a single

The Napier-Campbell Bluebird *in which its owner regained the land speed record in February 1931*

18

match, the telegram from Ramsay MacDonald, which stated, "I am glad to inform you that His Majesty King George V has been pleased to approve that the honour of Knighthood be conferred upon you". The following morning he returned to London in a private train called the "*Bluebird Special*", and the investiture took place two days later.

Maybe to celebrate his new found status, on 26th May Campbell placed his order with Thornycroft's for a new motor yacht, bigger than the first, and also to be called *Blue Bird*. At the time he declared that he had no intention of attacking the water speed record. Nevertheless, between 1937 and 1939 he was to break it four times, raising it to a creditable 142 m.p.h. In point of fact, the Rolls-Royce engine for the boat, in which he broke the record at 126 m.p.h. in 1937, was the same engine with which he achieved 301.13 m.p.h. on land on the Bonneville Salt Flats in Utah in 1935. He had the engine lifted out of the car and had a hull built around it.

As he was to have four similarly named motor yachts, to avoid confusion, I shall refer to them in this book as *Blue Bird 1*, formerly *Billduan*; *Blue Bird 2*, now *Bluebird of Chelsea*; *Blue Bird 3*, formerly *Frebelle III* and now *Chico*; and *Blue Bird 4*, now called *Blue Bird II*.

The "Bluebird Special" - the private train laid on to welcome Campbell back from Daytona

An impression of all the **Blue Bird** *yachts to show their comparative size and style*

19

Fun on the water. Boulter's Lock,
on Ascot Sunday, 19th June 1932

ACT TWO

The Carefree Thirties

"I believe we have the Blue Bird this time . . . The idea came to me like a ray from the sky, this morning only, when I recovered my strength in the dawn . . . we are at the entrance of the enchanted palaces where all men's joys, all men's happinesses are gathered together . . ."

Maeterlinck,   *The Blue Bird*

Sir Malcolm Campbell at Daytona on 7th March 1935 after he broke the world land speed record

This was an era when many elegant motor yachts were built by numerous boatyards all over the country, but it is difficult to say how much Campbell himself became involved with Thornycroft in the general design and layout of his new boat. It is a tribute to his energy and drive that on Monday 20th July, a mere fifty-five days after the order was placed, *Blue Bird 2* was launched by Dolly, then Lady Campbell, at Hampton Wick. In 1985-6 it took us about 355 days to complete her refit, but times and costs have changed dramatically. Len Cox, a naval architect and surveyor, who has known *Blue Bird* most of her life, was an apprentice at the time. The hours were long, a skilled shipwright could expect 1/7d (8p) per hour, and an apprentice $2^{1}/_{2}$d (1p) per hour. But what they did all enjoy was the satisfaction of learning a true craft. As he says, "At the end of one's time, you certainly knew your job and could look forward to never being out of work".

The men at Thornycroft's were certainly skilled craftsmen. Their new commission took shape with considerable speed but no loss of quality as the years were to prove. When she was surveyed half a century later, not a single one of her planks needed to be replaced, even if much else did.

Blue Bird 2 was to be 52' long with a beam of 11' and a 4' 6" draft. Her hull was of double-skin mahogany on Canadian Rock Elm frames. She was powered by two 50 h.p. Thornycroft 4-cylinder petrol engines with reducing reversing gear,

The interior of **Blue Bird 2** *being built at Thornycroft's yard showing her double mahogany-on-elm construction*

23

The hull complete and wheelhouse being fitted

bringing the propeller speed down to about half that of the engine. The petrol was stored in two 100 gallon tanks under the aft deck with an emergency supply forward of the cockpit: a great improvement on the virtually open steering shelter of *Billduan*. With a consumption of about eight gallons per hour at a speed of around 10 knots, this *Blue Bird* could run for a full day - some 240 nautical miles - without re-fuelling.

She was given a straight stem and stern with clean lines. Though she was cosy enough below, there were few comforts above deck. The original deck was covered with canvas, painted to keep the water out, but sometime after the war she was given teak decks. These had deteriorated badly by the time we found her and, as with much of the woodwork on the boat, had to be replaced. On the poop deck, the dinghy was slung on quarter davits, but in a post-war refit it was slung aft and an outside steering position was fitted. But more of that later.

The boat's interior design was a marvel of compactness with the crew's quarters, as was the custom of the time, carefully separated from that of the owners. The crew's berths, heating, cooking and washing arrangements were not only self-contained, but also separated from the rest of the boat by a steel bulkhead with a watertight door. Their access to the deck, from these somewhat cramped quarters, was through a hatch so as to be as unobtrusive as possible.

The owner's eight-foot stateroom aft was elegant and spacious with five portholes and a dressing table between two berths flanked by wardrobes, all in mahogany. Entry was gained by a passage and companion way from the wheelhouse. To port there was a washroom containing the head, shower and wash basin and to starboard there was storage space and a linen cupboard. The wheelhouse itself was roomy, with sliding doors on each side and an ingenious sliding sunshine roof. There was a settee berth and two removable hatches to give access to the engine room below. For'ard of this was the saloon with four portholes and a skylight with louvered glass panels. Here in the saloon the furniture consisted of a dining table with a wrap-around seat, a writing table, sideboard and bookcase, again all made in mahogany. To port was another settee bed or captain's day bed. Throughout the boat, Campbell had ordered the upholstery to be in blue leather, but none of this had survived when we found her. Instead there was melamine, Formica and velour from a later restoration. Between the

A view from her straight transom, which shows her elegant tumblehome

saloon and crew's quarters, connected by a sliding door, was the galley and pantry with its refrigerator and paraffin stove and a third 'head' to port. Immediately to starboard was the oilskin locker and beyond that a single sleeping cabin with a dressing table and mahogany wardrobe. At something of a pinch, six or seven people could have been accommodated on the new *Blue Bird*.

25

Dolly Campbell posing for the cameras before launching Blue Bird *with the traditional bottle of champagne. To her left (with glasses) is James Wentworth-Day, Campbell's biographer*

On Monday 20th July 1931, *Blue Bird* was ready to be launched. Contemporary photographs show Dolly Campbell, wide eyed beneath her cloche hat, clutching her coat about her and seemingly enveloped by the fox furs around her shoulders, poised to release the bottle. Cameras clicked and flashed, illuminating the gloom of Thornycroft's shed and the barely concealed, roughly constructed dais, on which the little group were crammed. Around her, like bodyguards from a gangster movie, the men in three-piece suits and trilby hats shuffled nervously and looked around. Campbell selfconsciously held a cine-camera on his arm.

In the background, the workmen waited at a respectable and respectful distance. Those on board donned their caps and as the bottle was duly smashed, *Blue Bird* slipped gently backwards into the water. Then, turned by warps, poles and with the assistance of what must have been the yard's entire workforce, she was brought alongside and tied up.

Not everything was finished and it took a week before she was ready to leave for her speed trials in the Solent where she was logged at a maximum of 10.45 knots. Leo Villa recalls that the maiden voyage commenced on 28th July. "After spending most of the day in stowing away the gear and stores, we finally got off during the afternoon. Left Thornycroft's yard at Hampton Wick at 4.00 p.m. and arrived at Cadogan Pier at 6.45 p.m. We nearly had a

26

collision with a tug and barges at Chiswick New Bridge, but managed to go astern in time". Just as well, as Campbell had only recently become a member of the Royal Thames Yacht Club, and a collision on his maiden voyage would have been bad form.

In the years since I acquired *Blue Bird*, I have enjoyed the numerous little coincidences that seem to be connected with

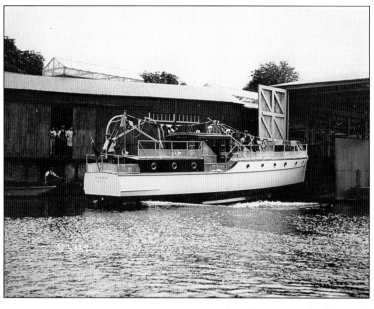

20th July 1931 and Blue Bird *enters the Thames at Hampton Wick for the first time*

her. Campbell and I share Pisces as a birth sign. He was 46 when he commissioned her and I was the same age when I bought her. She took 55 days to build, it was 55 years after

Thornycroft's watermen bring her alongside for final adjustments and fitting out

27

The owner and his wife aboard for the first time on a calm day with the Thornycroft builder's flag and bunting hanging limply from the halyards

her original launch in 1931 that I relaunched her as *Bluebird of Chelsea* in 1986, and in the street where I live my house is No. 55. Similarly she went to Cadogan Pier on both her maiden cruises and the earliest photograph of her underway is taken from exactly where she is moored now, on Cadogan Pier, looking towards Battersea Park. Some things are meant to be.

A month after Campbell took possession of her, on the August Bank Holiday Monday, *Blue Bird* was involved in the dramatic rescue of her owner. He and two of his friends, Capt. Millward and Capt. Davies, had just finished lunch at Beaulieu, when their attention was drawn to two men who appeared to be in difficulties in a small boat about a mile out to sea. They set out in a dinghy, rowing toward two holidaymakers caught in the off-shore current with the sea turning rough. An attempt at a tow failed but they got both men aboard before they too were swamped and potentially in great danger. Five men might easily have lost their lives that day, had not a girl on shore realised their situation and swum out to *Blue Bird*, who

had been anchored off-shore with the crew aboard. She and a young man who had followed her alerted Leo Villa and the crew, and *Blue Bird* went quickly to her owner's aid.

On 12th September Campbell, with a party of fifteen including Adm. Nicholson, Lady Drogheda, and Dolly, plus four crew, once again went to witnesss the Schneider Cup race. Earl Howe was to have been with them but had apparently crashed on his way from London.

The following summer, *Blue Bird* was entered in the London to Cowes race, although in that year it was held

Blue Bird *undergoing speed trials on the Thames, at the beginning of August 1931*

This picture shows (left to right) Admiral Wilmot Nicholson, Sir Malcolm Campbell and Doctor Benjafield aboard **Blue Bird,** *10th July 1932*

over a shortened course of two hundred miles from Rochester to Poole. She won an award for the best kept log, but nearly failed to finish as Campbell ran her aground at the entrance to Poole Harbour. It would seem that Campbell trusted his own judgement in navigation more than that of the illustrious crew of the day, which consisted of his father - the holder of a Board of Trade Master's Certificate - as well as a retired admiral of World War I and a Trinity House Pilot. However, all was well and she came off the sandbank quite quickly and finished fourth out of twelve.

Dolly seems to have enjoyed this *Blue Bird* much more than the first and regretted that, because of the children, she could not be included in more of the regular weekend cruises. "I used to feel", she wrote, "that he preferred to take his pleasures in his own way, but I always felt a degree of disappointment at being so consistently left out".

By 1933 Campbell, a restless man, was already thinking of a bigger boat. He had become increasingly nervous about the danger from the petrol engines and even considered changing them. He installed the latest fire-fighting equipment. Once, a prophetic gypsy had told him that tragedy would come from the water and

Sir Malcolm Campbell and friends in Blue Bird's *dinghy. Salcombe, Devon, 6th August 1932*

according to Campbell folklore, after he had a nightmare in which everyone on board died, following a petrol explosion, he sold her.

There is no doubt that Campbell much enjoyed *Blue Bird* and admired her sleek lines, reminiscent of a World War I Motor Gun Boat. His enthusiasm was not always echoed by Leo Villa, a landlubber by nature, whose son recalls, "he never wanted to go. I don't think he liked the boat very much, and he would have preferred to have no part of it. But I don't think that Malcolm Campbell was the kind of man you argued with, and so my father did as he was told and disappeared weekend after weekend". Len Cox, who was to survey her over forty years later, said that in her early days, *Blue Bird* was very much a man's boat, with only the bare necessities. Happily all that has now changed.

Whilst Sir Malcolm was enjoying *Blue Bird 2*, the Scottish yard of James N. Miller & Sons Ltd. at St. Monance, Fife, were building a motor yacht which began life as *Frebelle III*. She was destined to become another *Blue Bird*. She was a Watson of Glasgow design, built for Frank Bevan: 73' long with a 16' beam and a draft of 8'. When Campbell heard of her she was about six months old and for sale at Blythe, Northumberland at little more than £7,000. An altogether more substantial vessel than anything Campbell had previously

Blue Bird, *showing her paces on the River Thames*

31

Blue Bird 3 *in 1935, three years after she was built in Scotland*

owned - and she was to be his within six months - she was made of pitch pine on oak with a copper sheathed bottom and displaced 79.5 tons. *Frebelle III* was powered by two 80 h.p. Gleniffer diesel engines with twin screws and was the first Campbell boat which, like Lee Guinness' *Adventuress,* had a large funnel amidships. This released the exhaust gases and housed the freshwater tank.

But it was the comparative opulence below which made all the difference and probably gave Campbell the taste which he was to express in his last motor yacht some six years later. *Blue Bird 3* had a superb arrangement of staterooms and cabins; spaciousness for both owner and crew. Leo Villa recalled: ". . . an elegant saloon, a well-equipped galley with coal-fired heating and a practical engine room with workbenches and a 240v. alternator". She could accommodate ten guests and two crew in luxury. *Blue Bird 3* raised all their spirits including those of

Dorothy even though she did not expect any more involvement than on previous occasions. She realised that at least here was a comfortable vessel for both crew and passengers. Had Campbell perhaps understood that austerity for the crew and inexperience at the top was a recipe for mutiny? *Blue Bird 3* was certainly an improvement on her predecessor, but three years and two motor yachts had still failed to make a yachtsman of their owner, even if they had served to increase his enthusiasm.

Blue Bird 2's first owner after Campbell was D. D. Capper of Walton-on-Thames, in Surrey. He also had an address in Belfast, and was a member of Glasgow's Royal Clyde Yacht Club. Capper had the boat briefly in 1933/4, but nothing is known of him or where *Blue Bird 2* was kept at that time. But he could hardly have owned her for a year. He was followed in ownership by an archetypal Englishman. Captain Howard G. Picton-Davies came from a traditional military family. Generations of its sons served in the Royal Welch Fusiliers, and his grandfather took part in the Seige of Lucknow during the Indian Mutiny in 1857. Picton-Davies himself entered the Great War as a regular soldier and was badly wounded during action in France. The Ministry of War sent Howard home to what was confidently expected to be his deathbed. But the young captain confounded them all. He was invalided out of the service and never fully recovered; but despite his wounds and the loss of one kidney, he led an active post-war business and social life.

Picton-Davies set up as a solicitor in Weston-Super-Mare, Somerset, where all his life he continued to enjoy the reputation of a war hero. He was a charming, debonair character of considerable means, much admired locally for his generous disposition and - as the novelty of the talking pictures gripped and held cinemagoers - his film star looks. Living beside the sea, Howard and his wife, Una, took an

33

THE LYMINGTON SHIPYARD,
LYMINGTON, HANTS.
(MANAGING DIRECTOR—H. G. MAY)
Telephone 3.   Telegrams : "Yachts, Lymington."
FOR SALE
T.S. MOTOR CRUISER, 52ft. × 11ft.
Beam, with 6ft. 3in. Headroom. Built by
THORNYCROFT, 1931. Double skin
Mahogany. Excellent job. Chromium Fit-
tings. Electric Light Set. Thornycroft
R.D.4 Petrol Engines.
Collective H.P. 100. Speed 11 Knots.
Double Cabin, Single do. Large Deckhouse
with sliding roof. Very comfortable Saloon
entered from Deckhouse.
Plunge and Shower Bath, 3 w.c.'s. Fo'c'sle
and Galley for crew of two. 6 Berths ex. crew.
NOW IN COMMISSION.
PRICE **£1,750**
INSPECTION IN SOLENT BY ARRANGEMENT.

Blue Bird *for sale in 1933, when she was only two years old*

Captain Picton-Davies

interest in boats. He bought a one-time Burnham-on-Sea lifeboat, then renamed *Burnlibo*, which he kept at Buckler's Hard in the care of an Irishman called Rooney and his wife.

Then in 1934 he was attracted to a Thornycroft motor cruiser which H. G. May had for sale at his Lymington Shipyard. Strangely, the advertisement made no attempt to cash in on the fame of the boat's original owner, who by now had held the land speed record seven times and had recently won The Segrave Trophy. This was awarded annually, except for the war years, to 'the British subject who accomplishes the most outstanding demonstration of the possibilities of transport by land, air or water'. Malcolm was to win it again in 1939, and his son Donald received it four times, in the end posthumously. But in 1934 Mr May said of *Blue Bird* that her original petrol engines could generate 100 h.p. and achieve a speed of 11 knots, and she was an 'excellent job'. She certainly looked good in his advertisement, thrusting out at the reader, and Picton-Davies bought her for £1,750. Quite incidentally at that time he had to find a new ship's bell for his new boat. Each of Campbell's *Blue Birds* had, in turn, the same bell. When he parted with *Blue Bird 4*, his last ship, Leo Villa finally took down the bell and kept it among his treasures. Eventually it was passed on to his friend Paul Foulkes-Halbard who keeps it with his other "Campbell memorabilia" at Filching Motor Museum in Sussex.

Under Capt. Picton Davies' ownership, for the first time *Blue Bird* became truly a family boat. Her owner was not very adventurous and it is unlikely that he ever took *Blue Bird* abroad. She was used for short, gentle trips, for picnics and teas and weekend parties. Howard and Una delighted in having their family and friends on board, and the furthest west she is known to have sailed was to Exmouth where the Picton-Davies family had friends. On all these occasions they were looked after by Rooney and his wife, who made the food and waited on the ship's company. Douglas Hannah, Picton-Davies' nephew and then a teenager going down with his brother Peter from Kent or Sussex to their uncle's boat, still recalls the pleasure of those holidays and the excitement of being on one of Malcolm Campbell's former boats. "Campbell was at the height of his popularity. I remember we used to buy comics which offered a succession of *Blue Birds* as little cardboard cut-out models. Mother was not too keen on them so I never did complete my set. But we all knew that uncle's motor yacht had belonged to the fastest man on land and that was a great thrill".

Rooney, who looked after boats at Buckler's Hard

Rooney made tiny models for a hobby, and during this time fashioned and painted a minute likeness of *Blue Bird* in a matchbox. The Rooneys lived in a rented cottage at Buckler's Hard, and frequently stayed on the boat. Douglas Hannah recalls that they made their quarters not for'ard, as was intended for the crew in Campbell's original plan, but in the double sleeping cabin aft.

During his short period of ownership Picton-Davies took *Blue Bird* to the speedboat races organised by Ross Fedden in Poole harbour. This fired his imagination, and for a while he toyed with the idea of replacing the dinghy which *Blue Bird* carried on her aft deck and towed behind her when in motion, with a speed boat. But these plans were not to be realised. Captain Howard Picton-Davies' fortunes took a downward turn and *Blue Bird 2* had

Rooney's matchbox model of Blue Bird

35

to go. In 1937 she was once again for sale, but before *Blue Bird 2* meets her last private owner of the 1930s, we must return once more to Malcolm Campbell, for around this time he had an interest in two more boats, one of which we shall meet again - with *Blue Bird 2* and *Blue Bird 3* - during the evacuation from Dunkirk.

Whilst Capt. Picton-Davies was enjoying one of his former boats, Malcolm Campbell came to the end of his ownership of *Blue Bird 3* and for the moment financed a motor yacht conversion which was not for himself. During the 1930s he had been patron of the Carshalton Sea Scouts, led by Cdr. Freddie Clarke who started a Sea Cadet Corps at the beginning of the war. In 1936 Tough's converted for their use a former naval pinnace, some 40' long which had a large, copper funnel for'ard and was powered by triple expansion steam engines. Dorothy named her *Lady Campbell* at the Ferry boatyard, and there the boat stayed for the boys to take her on frequent trips to the Medway. The Sea Scouts were thrilled to be going on one of Campbell's boats with express permission of their patron, and such proximity to the great man gave rise to much hero-worship amongst jealous friends!

By the time war broke out, she had been renamed *Monarch*, and was immediately and not surprisingly commandeered by the Admiralty. They took her back to Tough's in 1942 to have her steam engines replaced by diesels, and she was certainly moored at Teddington in 1946. What happened to her after that is unknown, but she did not go back to the Carshalton Sea Scouts. After the war, they were to have the use of Cdr. Clarke's own motor yacht, *Lady Gay* which had been to Dunkirk and, now named *Mehatis*, is still with us.

In 1931 Malcolm Campbell wrote *My Greatest Adventure* about searching for pirate treasure on Cocos

36

Island. He wrote a second book: *Drifting To War* in 1937. Both of these titles were relevant to the last of the motor yachts he was to own before the outbreak of war. His 1931 *Blue Bird* changed owners for the third time, and became the property of a bailiff, working for the Wills family on the Littlecote estate in Berkshire. The one-time *Frebelle III* was with the Countess of Onslow at Blythe. And up at Humberside the Goole Shipbuilding & Repairing Company was putting together a vessel which, Sir Malcolm Campbell hoped, would help him realise his greatest dream.

Campbell had commissioned G. L. Watson's, the Scottish naval architects, to design a craft which would take him once again on a great treasure hunt to Cocos Island in the Pacific: Robert Louis Stevenson's famous Treasure Island. He had benefited from a substantial legacy which, since it was unexpected, might justifiably be put to this extravagant use. Besides, might it not allow him the long-desired opportunity and means of fulfilling a life-long ambition? When men of vision are given sufficient resources, their heart will invariably rule their head. Watson's came up with a boat just under 104' in length which fitted the owner's requirements for an ocean-going vessel able to stand up to the Atlantic crossing. The new *Blue Bird* displaced 175 tons and had a bow profile reminiscent of the *Queen Mary*. To the little Goole yard, whose fishing boats were their bread and butter work, so prestigious a boat for so eminent a person must have been the source of great pride.

The new *Blue Bird* was twice the length of the 1931 motor cruiser, with nearly $7^{1}/_{2}$ times the displacement, and was built for a specific purpose. In just seven years the man who once said he had 'no love for the sea' and that 'he hated it and really had some little fear of it', at least seems to have come to terms with it perhaps because it offered him a new

Blue Bird 4 *under construction at Goole*

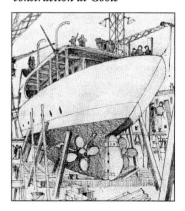

37

challenge. Biographers have speculated on Malcolm Campbell's acquisitiveness as a motivating factor throughout his life and indeed both his dream of a treasure island and that of owning an exquisite vessel might have helped him to overcome his fears.

In any event *Blue Bird 4*, launched in 1938, was the latest reincarnation of the name. Campbell went for space, comfort and power. The upper deck could take four ship's boats. Initially these were a 19' Chris Craft, a 16' Sea Joker, a 14' sailing dinghy and a 12' dinghy. Her whole line was rakish yet elegant with a high teak wheelhouse, an engaging

Blue Bird 4, *the largest of Campbell's cruisers, pictured in 1938*

funnel just behind and two beautifully proportioned masts.

The men at Goole could never before have worked on such a luxury design, and they were not to do so again. *Blue Bird 4* had five double cabins with en suite bathrooms, including Sir Malcolm's stateroom, as well as space in the fo'csle for a crew of five. The dining room was panelled in English oak, the smoking room in walnut. Each of her cabins was in a different wood and her twin Rushton diesel engines could generate 300 h.p., giving *Blue Bird* 11.75 knots or a cruising speed of 10 and a range of 5,000 miles. Cocos Island may not have seemed so far away.

But at the time Campbell had other, more pressing commitments. *Blue Bird 4* was delivered at the start of the season at a time when her owner was heavily involved with the water speed record. Lago Maggiore, Italy, saw him attain 128.30 m.p.h. on 1st September, 1937 and 129 m.p.h. the next day. A year later, on 4th September, he achieved 130.94 m.p.h. at Lake Halliwill, Switzerland and on 19th August 1939, 141.74 m.p.h. became the new record on Coniston Water in England. With all the

In two years immediately before the war Sir Malcolm Campbell improved on the water speed record in three different countries

preparations for these, coupled with the onset of war and numerous other commitments arising from the problems of the time, Malcolm Campbell never had enough opportunities to enjoy this *Blue Bird* fully and he managed only a few outings on her around the south east coast before war broke out. *Blue Bird* was requisitioned by the Royal Navy, and by the time it was all over Sir Malcolm Campbell was a sick man, and Treasure Island was beyond his reach. He died in 1948.

Capt. A. L. C. Fuller

In 1937 Picton-Davies sold *Blue Bird 2* to 48-year-old Capt. Arthur Loraine Claude Fuller, a former regular soldier. Fuller was commissioned in the 3rd/6th Dragoon Guards in 1913, finished the war as a gunnery instructor with the Royal Fusiliers and then spent some time teaching aerial gunnery in the U.S.A. In 1920 he was employed at Littlecote Manor, Berks. as tutor to George Seton Wills to whom he was later godfather. He took on the role of secretary to Sir Ernest Wills and eventually became estate manager.

Fuller lived with his wife and two children at Furze Coppice in Savernake Forest where he created an enviable garden. He was a very lively, funny and goodhearted man who raced horses, went tunny fishing in the North Sea and was President of the British Tunny Club. But he was also a considerable gambler.

Blue Bird 2 was to be the family's boat for under two years. She was kept at Poole and made only a few fairly local trips, for Mrs Fuller did not enjoy sailing. The boat was at Salcombe, Devon when war was declared in 1939, and the Navy took her over at once and kept her for the duration. Meanwhile Fuller himself fell out of favour at Littlecote early in the 1940s, moved to Sonning near Reading and tried his hand at pig farming, fruit farming and market gardening but none were financially successful.

Blue Bird *2 in 1939*

When *Blue Bird 2* was offered back to him at the end of the war he refused her, preferring to accept compensation and leaving the Ministry of War Transport to dispose of the boat.

ACT THREE

For King And Country

*"... What times we live in! ...
I never have a moment's peace.
I cannot understand Man,
these last few years. What is he
aiming at? ... As they are
children, we must give them
such a fright that they will not
dare to persist ..."*

Maeterlinck,   *The Blue Bird*

THE LITTLE BOATS OF ENGLAND

The little boats of England, the little motor-boats,
The little penny-steamers from Land's End to John o' Groat's,
The Brighton Belle, the Margate Queen, the Vigilant, the Lark,
The Saucy Jane, the Gracie Fields, even a Noah's Ark,
Picked up their country's message that its back was to the wall.
"There is danger, there is danger, will you answer to the call"?
And Francis Drake and Collingwood and Nelson of the Nile
Were on their quarterdecks again, you should have seen them smile
When all the little boats pushed out, from Dover to Dunkirk
To bring the British Army home, that was their job of work.
How they performed their fearful task, the epic of those days,
The history books will tell our sons, but let us sing their praise
And as they lie at anchor from Newcastle to Poldhu,
With their battle scars upon them, with their pennants red and blue,
We say to them with grateful hearts "Nelson is proud of you".

(. . . from a 1942 newspaper cutting)   ***IVOR BACK***

42

There is a strange irony in the fact that Campbell's *Blue Bird* motor yachts went to their most dangerous and exciting voyages after his ownership. On 14th May 1940 the BBC broadcast a message which was to relieve many owners of their vessels, for a number of years if not for ever. *The Admiralty have made an order requesting all owners of self-propelled pleasure craft between 30' and 100' in length to send all particulars to the Admiralty within 14 days from today if they have not already been offered or requisitioned.*

The Little Ships off Dover

The Admiralty had commandeered some private vessels at the beginning of the war for such duties as contraband control. They were proving both successful and necessary as naval auxiliaries under the command of the Royal Navy. Their roles were permanent enough to change their names in instances where the Navy already had craft with a similar name. Now boats were needed for harbour services and general patrol duties. When the evacuation of Dunkirk became necessary two weeks after the BBC announcement, the Admiralty had at least a growing cache of private craft to call upon, and a much better knowledge of where they could lay their hands on others in a hurry.

On 26th May the War Office alerted the Admiralty to the possibility of a mass emergency evacuation of the beleaguered British Expeditionary Force from France, by means of a secret cipher telegram. The Vice-Admiral Dover, from where 'Operation Dynamo' was to be controlled, began to mobilise the Little Ships already under his command. All around the coast boatyards and agents were officially telephoned and told to collect together all shallow-draft vessels in their vicinity. There was no time to consult or make prior arrangements with owners, many of whom heard about it for the first time when their boats had gone. At Poole in Dorset, where *Blue Bird 2* spent a great part of her life, Reg Yebsley of Elkins' boatyard had been ordered to stand by with a number of vessels which the Admiralty's requisitioning officer had already earmarked. Further west, Bernard Bradford was called upon to take Exmouth and Lympstone boats to Dartmouth, and much the same picture unfolded around the south and south east coasts.

Ron Lenthal had to collect the boats for Tough Brothers of Teddington, charged with providing the Thames flotilla which eventually numbered over one hundred Little Ships. For a fortnight boats on nearby moorings had to be kept ready, but without their batteries, to prevent their use by enemy agents. Ten days before the evacuation the word was given to commandeer any other suitable craft, and Ron searched everywhere to requisition boats and collect them at Teddington. All these were then taken in convoy to Ramsgate, to join those already acquired by the Navy.

And what of the *Blue Birds* at this point in time? *Blue Bird 1* had temporarily been lost sight of. *Blue Bird 2* had already been acquired by the Ministry of War Transport from Capt. A. L. C. Fuller. She was a late acquisition, no doubt earmarked specifically for the evacuation. *Blue Bird 3* had been requisitioned from the Countess of Onslow. On 28th December 1939 her registration was cancelled and she was placed on service with minelayers. Camper & Nicholson fitted her with echo sounding gear at Gosport; she was renamed *Chico* in January 1940, commissioned on 6th March and based at Dover after a period at Brightlingsea.

Wherever the requisitioned boats were - and most of those used were from the Thames and Medway areas with a few around the south coast - they were collected, serviced and towed in convoy to collection points and ultimately to Ramsgate. Most were then towed or they went under their own steam to Dunkirk with naval officers or ratings in charge, though some had volunteer civilian crews; rarely did the owners go. In some respects the Admiralty had been over-optimistic about their new resources. Little flotillas of boats were prepared all around the south coast, taken to a central point, then returned home the next day when it became clear that events at Dunkirk were progressing too rapidly for them to make the journey in time. This situation has always given rise, in later years, to the honest but mistaken belief that particular vessels actually took part in the evacuation, when in fact they got no closer than the intention to do so. In the event, however, at least 640 vessels which collectively have become known as The Little Ships of Dunkirk took part. No one knows the exact number, for some were not officially requisitioned. They were hastily got together with civilian crews and patriotic owners and went to sea, anxious to contribute to the desperate effort.

A flotilla of Little Ships collected on the Thames, being towed away to war

In some cases the departure of these boats was not properly recorded in the confusion of the moment, and we know of them only because of some incident which occurred once they had left Ramsgate. For the others, the majority, it was a matter of reporting at Sheerness, where civilian crews enlisted for the operation and fuel and provisions were put on board, then off to Ramsgate - last stop before Dunkirk.

If the authorities were having problems coping with the boats they knew about from the very beginning, matters only got worse. As the evacuation proceeded and supplies dwindled, other little ships which had not been requisitioned turned up and more people than they could cope with volunteered to crew them. Elsewhere things were going better than expected. Winston Churchill believed at the outset of the operation that within a week he would be

45

reporting to Parliament "the greatest military disaster in our long history" and that only between 20,000 and 30,000 men would be saved. As it turned out, the Little Ships, working in conjunction with the larger naval vessels lying offshore and often with their own specific tasks to perform, helped to bring back 338,226 men between 26th May and 4th June. But as boat after boat came back and discharged its human cargo, the ships were checked in, re-fuelled, given more provisions and sent off again. In the midst of all this frantic activity, *Blue Bird 2* arrived.

She went to Dunkirk under the command of Lt. Col. H. T. B. Barnard TD, RA, then a 52-year-old veteran of World War I, in which he had served with the West Kent (Queen's Own) Yeomanry. His service included campaigns in Egypt, France and Palestine. In civilian life he was an architect and surveyor living in London, and was also a director of two armament companies. Since 1920 he had risen from the rank of lieutenant in the 6th Kent Field Brigade, Royal Field Artillery of the reconstructed Territorial Army, and for barely three years before Dunkirk had been on the T.A.'s reserve list of officers.

Harold Barnard was himself a yachtsman, and therefore a good choice of skipper for such a boat as *Blue Bird*. Many of the Little Ships were going across the Channel with civilian crews who were used to this type of craft, but under the command of naval personnel who were not. However, Barnard knew his boat and also the Channel. Even so, it was not until *Blue Bird's* third attempt, on Sunday 2nd June, that she made it. Her first was thwarted due to engine failure at Lowestoft, where she had been on coastal patrol. Her second attempt out of Sheerness was abandoned because of 'an excess of volunteers'. By now, the secret which the collecting boatyards had kept for a fortnight, was well and truly out, and the authorities were

46

having problems not just with people offering their boats, but by the numbers of volunteer crews.

Finally, with a chosen complement of yachtsmen and naval ratings, *Blue Bird* successfully reached the starting line at Ramsgate. There, naval officers handed out orders and details of the route to be followed. Fuel, water and provisions - enough for two days - were put aboard from massive stockpiles. Little convoys of vessels were assembled and sent on their way. At 8 o'clock in the evening on a calm summer's day, in good light, *Blue Bird* headed for Dunkirk together with H.M. schuit *Rika* - a commandeered Dutch coaster. She was late in the operation to be making a first voyage, and it was late in the day. At least this meant a fairly uneventful trip under cover of darkness when the enemy dive bombers were much less active.

Many of the small craft involved, having been requisitioned by the Admiralty for auxiliary naval duties from the beginning of the war, took part in 'Operation Dynamo' painted in battleship grey. Others had their name plates painted out which - even if anyone was actually concerned at the time - made the identification of many vessels difficult if not impossible. Actual sightings during the evacuation are understandably few. However, Vic Vasey then a 20-year-old yachting engineer en route for Dunkirk from the River Hamble via Dover, recalls coming across *Blue Bird* in convoy on her outward journey.

Vic had sailed out of Southampton at 5 o'clock in the morning in a flotilla of thirteen ships; an unlucky number, for one caught fire and was destroyed off Brighton. In the middle of the Channel that evening, he came across *Blue Bird* going the same way. "You didn't see many names" he said, "and coming across this one with her name written across her stern and the little birds on the bows, had such a nice feel about it". Vic had never seen the Blue Bird play, yet he felt "it was a happy name, and it struck me enough to remember it ever afterwards". He also remembered the lines of the boat which he trailed across the Channel. When, nearly half a century later, Vic saw *Bluebird of Chelsea* for the first time since Dunkirk in a lock on the Thames near Taplow, Buckinghamshire, he recognised her at once.

As he crossed the Channel, Barnard had time to reflect on the best way he could use his boat. His orders had not been as specific as some; he was not carrying provisions or ammunition for the troops, expecting at any moment to make a last stand against the enemy on the ground at Dunkirk. Passing in the opposite direction, on their way back to Dover, and seemingly oblivious to the effects of their wash on the small craft struggling to get across, were the

Blue Bird *in action at Dunkirk*

naval destroyers and commandeered passenger vessels. They ploughed vast watery furrows, packed to the last inch with men and dangerously low in the water. *Blue Bird* might be able to work out to one of these, lying offshore. And if she survived, she could fill up with men and bring them home.

With a draft of 4'6", *Blue Bird* was rather more restricted in what she could do than the shallow draft and therefore more suitable vessels. She could not get very close to the beaches, although Barnard tried at first. But this was near the end of the evacuation. The dead, felled by constant enemy attack from the air over the previous few days, or blown out of their rescue boats and floated ashore, were still being buried by volunteers. Otherwise the beaches had been more or less cleared. Troops arriving now preferred to take their chances in the harbour of Dunkirk. Barnard found no men waiting to be rescued from the eastern end of the beaches, so he too made for the harbour. He knew that *Blue Bird* would be able to take troops from the jetty or the makeshift piers of lorries and bren gun carriers which had been driven into the water, sometimes on top of each other, to form landing stages for boats of deeper draft.

Conditions in and around the harbour were appalling, and proved difficult enough even for experienced crews to navigate. The sea had turned to a black, treacly oily mixture; the air as dense and fume-laden as a man could tolerate with difficulty. The harbour was full of sunken wrecks; the advancing Germans had recently got its range and shrapnel from shells was flying around. Stray tow ropes, the debris from vessels blown out of the water and reduced to pieces, fuel drums, floating human bodies and limbs, and innumerable discarded items of clothing including heavy greatcoats were all potential hazards. The boats themselves, jostling for position, being overrun and occasionally overturned by too many eager evacuees, were sometimes just

Douglas Hannah (fourth from left, top row) nephew of one-time Blue Bird *owner Howard Picton-Davies was himself rescued from Dunkirk*

as much a danger to each other. And from above came the constant bombardment from the air: strafing the embarkation points, bombing the Little Ships and screaming out to sea to engage and sink the larger vessels packed solid with men. Whenever a laden troopship set off, German aircraft screamed into the attack and the crew of many a Little Ship as it sailed back through the carnage saw the men it had just rescued and placed on board back in the water.

Blue Bird cautiously edged her way through all this; Barnard, inspired by his military training, and the crew by that extra strength one often gets when all appears to be lost, persevered. But it was a near thing. On one trip to the jetty something fouled the boat's propellers and the engines stopped. This was cleared, but shortly afterwards, whilst topping up, it was discovered that water had been put into her petrol tank. This was not an uncommon occurrence during 'Operation Dynamo', and was caused by pressure of time and by inexperience. Back at Sheerness and Ramsgate

50

they had used up all their water containers quite early in the evacuation and substituted empty petrol cans. Although appropriately marked, when handed out at speed, often in the dark, the substitution was frequently overlooked until it was too late. The boats, like *Blue Bird,* were in the thick of it when their engines failed and had either to be abandoned or towed back.

Not for the last time in her life did it seem that *Blue Bird's* days were over. Her engines dead, her propellers fouled, she lay disabled - as much a piece of debris as the other remains of battle around her. Perhaps in non-military hands she would have been given up for lost at that point and abandoned. But along came the Dutch schuit *Hilda* which had survived Dunkirk since she became involved at the outset of the evacuation. Barnard threw a line, and *Blue Bird 2* was towed back.

After Dunkirk, *Blue Bird* was taken up for service by the Admiralty as a radar decoy ship, operating out of Plymouth on runs between Gosport and Weymouth. For some inexplicable reason she seems to have avoided any damage and survived remarkably intact. When Pat McNaughton came across her in 1941 she still looked like an elegant river cruiser and had her complete inventory of crockery and her cutlery embellished with the bluebird emblem.

Other requisitioned boats were stripped of non-essential equipment such as crockery and cutlery, which were stored by the boatyard, pending their return, or collection by the owner. How had *Blue Bird* fared so well in naval hands and why had Captain Fuller not removed them?

The Dutch schuit Hilda *towing* Blue Bird *home*

51

Pat McNaughton had a particular interest in *Blue Bird 2*. Brought up around Lakes Windermere and Coniston before the war he had trained as a marine engineer with Campbell & Isherwood at Liverpool. After being evacuated from Dunkirk, he came home on the *Crested Eagle*, a Thames Service Ship which was bombed and sunk on 29th May 1940 with heavy loss of life. Later he went on an officer training course at Bournemouth, at the end of which they were all asked whether anyone had experience of small boats. Pat had, and found himself spending most of his war service with the Royal Army Service Corps as a workshop officer in a water transport company based at Plymouth.

He was there when *Blue Bird* was taken over by the R.A.S.C. from the Royal Navy. She was in beautiful condition, her wooden hull was undamaged, her topsides were well varnished and her chrome sparkled. She was immediately covered in regulation grey paint and spent the rest of the war transporting supplies from her base at Plymouth. The other main function of the Water Transport section of the R.A.S.C. was to tow practice targets for the coastal Royal Artillery gunners. *Blue Bird* escaped this as she was considered to be too slow.

Saved from target practice and enemy action, she still might not have survived. One day in 1943 the engines backfired whilst she was in Sutton Harbour, Plymouth. This set alight the contents of the bilges and while putting out the fire, Pat McNaughton inhaled more of the fumes than was good for him and landed in hospital. *Blue Bird* was put to rights and resumed her humdrum career in government service with no further mishaps.

Malcolm Campbell was by now a director of the Ford Motor Company and their subsidiary Lincoln Cars at Brentford, Middlesex. This part of the company imported the American Mercury and Lincoln Continentals for sale in Britain, but during World War II serviced tanks and bren gun carriers. The general manager of Lincoln Cars from 1938 until he retired in 1955 was Alistair B. Macintosh, a former naval officer who had been through World War I. In 1950 he became the registered owner of *Blue Bird.*

Macintosh knew Campbell well, and from 1940 to 1946 had one of his record-breaking speed boats under canvas on a cradle beside the employees' bicycle shed at Lincoln Cars. It was *K3,* the craft in which Campbell clocked 141.74 m.p.h. at Coniston Water on 19th August 1939. She was then bought for £300 by another of Campbell's friends, car dealer John Simpson of Wembley, and Macintosh looked after her while he moved premises and got them in order.

Former apprentice Dick Sangster remembers the speedboat during this period, and how the apprentices used to sneak under the canvas to hide or to eat their sandwiches. Every so often someone from the factory was sent to tidy it up and do occasional cosmetic work. Once Mr Macintosh had the boat stripped of all its metal fittings which he sent away to be chromium plated. Bearing in mind this was wartime, it seems an odd thing to do. She lay beside the bicycle shed more or less undisturbed until March 1945 when one of the last enemy rockets to be fired landed on the adjacent Packard works. The boat was showered with heavy debris, sustaining considerable damage.

And what of the two later *Blue Bird*s which took part in the evacuation? *Blue Bird 3* had a particularly illustrious naval career. On 30th May 1940 she went to Dunkirk under the command of Sub-Lieut. J. Mason, RNVR, where she picked up 217 troops and came back to Dover. Next day she returned and ferried about 1,000 men between the shore and the larger ships waiting off. And

Enemy action which damaged K3 in 1945

53

Troops transferring from **Chico (Blue Bird 3)** *to a transport vessel*

Dive bombing **Chico**

when she arrived back at Dover for the second time, 100 grateful men stepped ashore. After a quiet day, now about midway through the evacuation, with the traffic and the carnage at its height, she was transferred to life-saving duties on Route X. This was the new middle route across the Channel, from the North Goodwin to the Ruytingen Pass and then into Dunkirk Roads.

In March 1941 she was involved in a fight with an enemy bomber off Dungeness, when attacked as one of a fleet of Little Ships under Dover Command. *Chico* is credited with shooting the tail off the aircraft. About a month later she was again bombed by enemy aircraft with British fighters in pursuit, and once more escaped. In May, in company with other vessels, *Chico* was carrying out routine maintenance on a buoy when the group was dive-bombed by two Dorniers. For the third time, *Chico*'s luck held. Indeed, her only damage of the war seems to have been self-inflicted, when she collided with some M.T.B. pens.

In January 1943 she had an engine overhaul at the London Graving Dock, Poplar, reallocated for service with the Royal Naval College, Greenwich and then transferred to the Medway Mine Watching Patrol at Chatham. For nearly two years she remained there without incident and was then laid up at Mears Yard, Twickenham under the Director of Sea Transport's care and maintenance arrangement. Her naval career came to an end when she was disposed of in August 1946.

    Blue Bird 4 also went to Dunkirk, although her part in the evacuation has never been recorded in detail. Requisitioned, like her predecessor right at the start of hostilities, she was used both by the Royal Navy and the Waterborne Division of the Army. Fitted with a machine gun, she had a varied career over the next seven years over a wide area on the western side of Britain. She spent some time at Rothesay on the Isle of Bute and in coastal waters around south west Scotland and the Irish Sea. She was used for navigational training, minesweeping, observation and general support work. *Blue Bird 4* also had a spell in the Liverpool area, variously engaged on work with H.M. Customs Examination Service, mine watching and watching out for approaching enemy vessels and aircraft. At one time, working out of Londonderry, Northern Ireland, she patrolled the coast of Eire intercepting 'neutral' cargo vessels. During this time the crew, all keen fishermen, ran a lucrative sideline in trolling for mackerel and selling their catch to the Irish.

        Only once did *Blue Bird 4* come near to danger. She narrowly missed being blown up by a bomb which, had it not failed to explode, would have put paid to the boat and its crew. But she did survive, and in 1946 Malcolm Campbell was offered her back and paid less than half the amount the Admiralty had paid when they requisitioned her. But her condition was poor, restoration would have cost thousands of pounds and Campbell soon tired of the project and sold her. His dream boat and his dream had gone.

Blue Bird 4, *armed with machine guns, on patrol in war time, 1941*

The end of the war. Winston Churchill is mobbed as V.E. Day is celebrated in London

ACT FOUR

The Years After

*"This is a great day, a day of days!
. . . He is seeking the Blue Bird,
whom you have kept hidden from
man, since the beginning of the
world and who alone knows our
secret. Yet he possesses a diamond
which has the virtue of setting free
our spirits for a moment . . ."*

Maeterlinck, *The Blue Bird*

Henley Royal Regatta, 1946
The Thames returning to
 its peace time aspect

58

When the Navy finished with *Blue Bird 2* in 1947 they were left with her on their hands. She was placed, along with a considerable number of other vessels which had been requisitioned and were no longer required by the immediate pre-war owners, in one of the Ministry of War Transport's several caches of boats for disposal. These repositories provided an instant market for dealers and members of the public, and amongst the former came T. W. Allen of East Molesey.

This firm still exists as a yacht and boat builder, charterer and Thames cruiser hire company, but in the late '40s Allen was just a yacht broker. During the war he had taken his business from 25, Haymarket, in the centre of London and moved to the river just out of town. He died in 1984 and his son, who now has the business, was only three years old when *Blue Bird* was being stripped of any remnants of war service at the Surrey yard, and restored to a suitable condition for river cruising.

There are no existing records of the work done by Allen's yard or the asking price for *Blue Bird*. However, David Grose, then just out of the Navy and starting up in business, recalls a figure of £5,000 when he took a fancy to her at Ash Island, had a test run on the Thames and tried unsuccessfully to agree terms with Allen. He also remembers that, whether attributable to Allen's good work or the Navy's uncharacteristically sympathetic handling, *Blue Bird* was in good shape and did not appear as if she had been through the ravages of Dunkirk or years of hostilities in the aftermath. And she still had the pair of 4-cylinder Thornycroft petrol engines which were to give another decade of service.

The man who eventually bought her from Allen's yard was R. G. Finch of Totteridge, London. He was to have her no longer than her immediate pre-war owner and, apart from the fact that he was a member of the Little Ship Club, nothing is known of him. Yet it was Mr Finch who was responsible for *Blue Bird's* first change of name; he called her *Bluefinch,* the title she was to carry for the next twenty-seven years.

Hardly a year passed after Mr Finch's purchase of *Bluefinch* before she was bought by a man who knew her first owner well and was himself connected with motor cars. Alistair B. Macintosh was General Sales Manager of Lincoln Cars Ltd. in the Great West Road at Brentford, Middlesex. He bought the boat in 1950 and took her to moorings at Tagg's Island, on the Thames west of East Molesey, where he had lived with his Scottish wife on a succession of boats since 1924. Tagg's Island, the eyot between the one on which *Bluefinch* was built and the one on which she began her post-war existence, also has a theatrical connection. It was here that Frederick Westcott, better known as Fred Karno, had his great theatre and casino leisure complex of which there is now hardly a trace.

Alistair B. Macintosh was born in Cambridge. At first he went into farming, was apprenticed at a foundry and completed his training at the Sunbeam Car Company's Wolverhampton works. Before World War I he had his own retail motor business in Canada, but when war broke out he sold up and booked a passage on the *Lusitania.* At the last moment he transferred to another ship and the *Lusitania* set off, to be sunk by a torpedo.

He married in 1913. Commissioned in the Navy the next year, he held flying certificates for both land and sea planes. After World War I he joined the Ford Motor Company at Regent Street in central London. All his life his friends included high ranking military men with whom he had influence. When one of his workers, Les Galloway, received Army call-up papers in 1944 and would have preferred the Navy, he took them to Macintosh who had them exchanged immediately.

Bespectacled, well over six feet tall and rarely seen without his trilby hat, Macintosh had the reputation of being a first-class and persuasive salesman. He became a sales rep. at Ford's subsidiary Lincoln Cars in 1930, was promoted to London Sales Manager in 1933 and always claimed that in 1934 he sold the first Lincoln car to come into Britain from the United States since before Prohibition. Just before World War II he was appointed General Sales Manager under the chairmanship of Sir Malcolm Campbell - another of those *Blue Bird* coincidences.

For many years the Macintosh family lived on the motor yacht *Gertrude Elizabeth*, and they had several more boats of their own. He was just five years off retirement when he bought *Bluefinch* in 1950, intending to do whatever was necessary and pass her on, having for many years run a sideline in yacht brokerage. It was his wife's job to keep their current boat and attend to the cosmetic side of those he bought for resale.

A member of both the Royal Thames Yacht Club and the Royal Corinthian Yacht Club, Macintosh was well known on the river. He was a friend of Douglas Tough of the Teddington firm and of Ron Lenthall their lighterman who collected together the Thames flotilla of Little Ships which took part in the Dunkirk evacuation. Tough sometimes had a boat which might interest him, and Ron delivered them to Tagg's Island for inspection. But he also had moorings at Burnham-on-Crouch, Essex and *Bluefinch* was taken there on her only voyage under Macintosh and put up for sale in 1952. When he retired from the motor trade, Macintosh took on the job of Moorings Manager at Tagg's Island.

Bluefinch was spotted by Cecil Carrington Loyst, a

man said to be a real boating fanatic with a passion for any craft which floated on the water. Sadly it was not an interest shared by his wife even though they lived for some time aboard a motor yacht called *Wilhelmine*, moored at Duck's Wharf.

Loyst was a Canadian who came to England from Toronto at the end of World War II. In partnership with two others he set up as a building contractor - Carrington's Building Construction - at Whitton, Middlesex. When he bought *Bluefinch* in 1953, he registered her at his business address in the name of his second wife Kay. The couple met on a cruise liner when they were both in their early 50s, and after their marriage lived together at Hove, Sussex. It was around the resorts of Brighton and Hove that *Bluefinch* was to spend the next three years of her life.

As the business took more of Mr Loyst's time, *Bluefinch* had less of it. She was brought back to Tagg's Island where she was more conveniently situated for living on during the business week. It was there, being used as a houseboat, that Ron Blindell found her for sale in 1956.

Ronald James Rae Blindell was an archetypal businessman. He was the successful son of a well-known family in trade, married a bright young debutante and enjoyed a life in which he could indulge his personal passions to the point of philanthropy whilst keeping his finger in many and varied business pies. Born in 1906, Ron was the son of James, later Sir

Bluefinch *moored as a houseboat at Tagg's Island in the mid 1950s*

James Blindell, Member of Parliament for Boston & Holland and Liberal Party Chief Whip in the 1930s.

Ron Blindell

He started work at the age of fifteen as errand boy in his father's one retail boot and shoe shop in Grimsby, Yorkshire. When James died in 1937, thirty two years before his son, Ron was the Managing Director of the business which then included thirteen shops. He made Blindell's Ltd. into a highly successful national retail chain of 130 shops with a manufacturing facility in Leicester and a flourishing export business.

During the war Blindell's supplied boots for the Army. I wonder if any weary feet were eased out of Blindell's footwear aboard *Blue Bird* during the evacuation from Dunkirk? Ron himself served in the Royal Artillery until discharged on medical grounds, when he became a volunteer fireman and later deputy fire chief of the Grimsby auxiliary fire service. It was also at this time that he established a link with the west country which was to develop in later years. The Imperial Hotel at Torquay, he always said, was the only place in the country where there was any decent night life during the war, and it was in that part of the world he spent some of his happiest times.

A Grimsby town councillor for many years, he also fought several post-war elections for the Liberals and then the Labour Party: Nottingham in 1945, Wellingborough in 1947 and Truro in 1959. Ron came to live at Anstey's Cove near Torquay and was briefly Chairman of Torquay United F.C. in the early 1950s. He went on to be Chairman at Plymouth Argyle (1958-64) and then Brentford where in 1967 he saved the club from a takeover by Queens Park Rangers by personally buying £40,000 worth of shares and lending the club a further £104,000 interest free. He was also owner of *Stalbridge Colonist*, the 1966 winner of the Hennessy Gold Cup.

63

When *Bluefinch* came into Ron's life the family lived at Mawnan, Cornwall, and he was preparing to fight the 1959 General Election at Truro for Labour.

Very little had been done to *Bluefinch* since Campbell's ownership. Ron had her substantially refitted and put in two 100 h.p. Perkins 56M diesels before moving her from the Thames. Kay Blindell still recoils in horror from the memory of that first voyage by sea towards Falmouth which was to be her home port. In their inexperienced hands, although they had a full-time skipper, it was like riding a roller-coaster. She pitched and rolled in a most disturbing way and the new owners were greatly alarmed by her apparent instability. Detained by fog and bad weather at Newhaven, Ron left for business reasons, the family went home by other means, and the skipper was left to complete the journey to Falmouth harbour.

Mrs Blindell remembers some wonderful times on *Bluefinch,* following the regattas around the harbours of Devon and Cornwall. They thought that *Bluefinch* was built for speed, not cruising, and never took her to sea. In fact once they had moved to Strete in Devon and secured a mooring opposite Dartmouth town, they dreaded leaving the sanctuary of the river. But when Ron fought for the Truro seat *Bluefinch* lay in a creek outside the town; her owner ferrying backwards and forwards in the dinghy. He had to endure many pointed remarks about a Labour candidate affluent enough to own a motor yacht!

Mostly *Bluefinch* went up and down the Dart between Dartmouth and Totnes where Ron owned the Seymour Hotel. They used the boat, according to Mrs Blindell, instead of a car. Just once were they stuck on the mud at low tide when, failing to heed their skipper's advice they delayed a journey. The poor skipper was greatly embarrassed by the little dinghies which kept floating up, asking whether they required a tow!

Christopher Best, Blindell's nephew, remembers being taken on board *Bluefinch* as a young lad. He stuck his head through a portlight and was jammed there for over an hour feeling very unwell and watching the water lurching up at him. Whilst the family enjoyed *Bluefinch* they were never fully at ease sailing her, and it is quite amazing that she stayed with them for about seven years. Eventually, with the boys away at school, they moved to Ascot and left the boat behind. In the hands of her next owner, *Bluefinch* nearly met a traumatic end.

The Dart is one of the most beautiful rivers in England. Two of the passenger vessels which now take tourists along its navigable length between Dartmouth and Totnes were at the beaches of Dunkirk with the *Blue Bird* motor yachts in 1940. Later, Donald Campbell was often to

River passenger vessels made good rescue boats at Dunkirk, and those which survived went back into service. Dartmothian *and* My Queen *still do daily trips along the Dart in Devon*

65

be seen on the river with his *Blue Bird* speed boats; an awesome spectacle for people in the area who remember it to this day. Halfway along the navigable river is Galmpton, which is where Torquay businessman Sidney R. Smith brought *Bluefinch* when he bought her in 1964.

Galmpton is near Torquay where Mr Smith became a member of the Royal Torbay Yacht Club, and very close to Dartmouth where he frequently used Dart Marina. From there he made numerous trips to the Channel Islands. Jim Anstey, who then lived at the marina, recalls how Mr Smith always liked to make an early morning start on these occasions. He was often raised from his bed at some late hour of the night to attend Mr Smith coming into the marina with *Bluefinch*, to fill her fuel tanks. According to Jim the coastguards became suspicious of *Bluefinch*'s frequent and apparently exclusive runs to the Channel Islands and began an investigation, but nothing came of it.

The boat survived the mid '60s by the narrowest chance. Moored by the south embankment at Sandquay, Dartmouth in 1966, *Bluefinch* blew up. Mr Smith was on board with a nephew when a match was struck which ignited a gas leak. The nephew was blown out of the hatch and Smith himself scrambled out very shaken. The nylon socks he had been wearing were virtually destroyed in the heat of the explosion and his nylon and wool sweater hung

The explosion which might have put an end to Bluefinch

about him like loose chainmail where the nylon fibres had all given way. Shards of glass embedded themselves in the brightwork of *Sparkle*, the Torbay pleasure boat which was alongside, and the force of the explosion scorched a nearby building. As for *Bluefinch*, her bows were blown apart, her foredeck ruptured and she - in the words of the marina's Managing Director at the time -

66

split like a pea pod lengthways, and immediately sank. Everyone concerned thought that would be her end.

The marina where the accident occurred, owned by Dart Marina Ltd., was run for their parent company by Tony Smith the Managing Director and no relation of the owner. He knew enough of her history to feel that this should not be her ignominious end. So he hauled *Bluefinch* out of the water. When she was pronounced lost for insurance purposes he called on the shipwrights at George Philip & Son - a local associated company in the Reeves merchant timber group - to see what might be done.

According to Tony, the wood of the hull was fairly sound, the original mahogany was soft in places, the deck had lifted, and every other part of the fabric was beyond repair. Mr Smith had replaced Ron Blindell's engines with a pair of 6-cylinder, 105 h.p. Perkins 6.354 complete with Borg-Warner oil operated reverse reduction gear boxes, providing handed rotation of her propellers. All this was intact. In the wheelhouse were the two plaques *Bluefinch* and *Dunkirk 1940*. As he picked them up Tony felt strangely moved, as if in that instant the whole of the boat's history reached out to him, and in so doing secured her future.

Bluefinch did not take much gutting because internally the explosion had done quite a thorough job. Dart Marina Ltd. rebuilt her exactly as she had been except for two things. They put in central heating in deference to prevailing taste in the mid '60s when boat owners required more warmth, and they altered the shape of the wheelhouse. Thornycroft's had built the then fashionable square pill-box arrangement in 1931, whilst the restoration put a 30 degree rake on the front.

Philips' shipwright joiner Ron Efford remembers how he spent a week fitting mahogany planking between the

Raised from the mud at Dartmouth, Bluefinch is inspected for damage caused by the explosion

Evidence of the vertical split at her bow

67

wheelhouse and the decking, and then went on to fit out the dining area in Formica. The new front of the wheelhouse was built of plywood and not mahogany boards like the rest of the structure. Wherever the mahogany needed replacing, such as beneath the aft window on the port side, plywood panels were used instead. It was much cheaper, of course, but future owners were to realise how much more varnishing was needed.

The whole job took almost a year to complete. Richard Primrose, the Brixham marine surveyor who had acted for the underwriters in Mr Smith's insurance claim, says that Dart Marina "did a really good job, making *Bluefinch* a basic but extremely sound boat". Her strength was soon to be put to the test.

Bluefinch's apparent demise was swift and violent. The story of her end in a peaceful marina followed close on the sound of the explosion which was heard all over the town. Once started, the tale, no doubt embellished with the telling, ran around Dartmouth almost as fast as the explosion had catapulted the boat's occupants into the air. The sinking of a well-known, much admired boat is always of great interest to those who know her and a matter of much speculation. It was said that Sidney Smith was something of an inventor, a rather mysterious person said to have filled his boat with strange gadgets, and that he had gone looking for a gas leak with a match! Poor Mr Smith could never have won; for whilst his own demise might have brought public sympathy, that of his boat invited scepticism.

But when such a boat is raised with good intentions, interest is locally rekindled. And when those intentions come together in practice, there is always much speculation on her future and a cautious jockeying for position amongst those who might be able to share in it. So it was with *Bluefinch*. When Dart Marina put her salvaged remains in a shed beside their moorings, Sidney and Valerie Osborne were by no means the only people to take an interest in what was going on.

Sidney Osborne, DFC had been a lucky young wartime Squadron Leader with Lancaster bombers. His love of flying was matched by his love of the sea. Both involve coming to terms with the elements. He was an excellent shot and fly fisherman who adored salmon fishing. Mrs Osborne preferred sailing, and they had a boat moored next to *Bluefinch*'s shed at Dart Marina. Unwilling at first to accept her husband's suggestion that they buy her, Valerie found herself "sneaking into the shed when no one was around, climbing the ladder, and having a good look at what was going on". The charm of *Bluefinch* was captivating.

This was the era of Formica and plastic; cheap, practical and easy to clean. Sheets of it went into the rebuilt *Bluefinch*, and whilst the men considered the workmanship of the restoration, the ladies kept an eye on the hygienic worktops going into the galley. When it was all finished, the Osbornes bought *Bluefinch*, "a delight to live on", which took them cruising for up to four weeks at a time over the next three years. In particular they often went to the Brittany coast, stopping off in the Channel Islands where Alderney was their favourite. It was in St. Helier harbour "where the tide disappears as quickly as if someone has pulled out the plug", that *Bluefinch* had to use her steadying legs. Once, at Fowey in Cornwall,

Bluefinch, *in Le Havre, newly rebuilt and under the Osbornes' ownership*

69

she suffered the phenomenon known as 'runaway diesels', when the engines could not be stopped until someone stuffed rags into *Bluefinch*'s exhausts. Just as in Mr Smith's case, the word quickly went around the town about 'the yacht that caught fire' to the great embarrassment of the owners who heard the story being told in the local pub!

Indeed, *Bluefinch* continued her charmed life. Moored one night in the River Fal against concrete barges left from the war, next to a friend's 48' Dutch steel-hulled boat, they both went aground. Gradually *Bluefinch* took the whole weight of her heavy neighbour and for two-and-a-half hours before the tide turned, remained in imminent danger of being pushed over and crushed into the mud. Yet, a testimony to her sturdy rebuilding, she withstood all the pressure. Only a rail broke under the strain before the tide came back and lifted the boats apart.

After about three years, Sidney Osborne's eye was caught by a larger boat which he thought might be more sea-worthy, and *Bluefinch* was put up for sale at Dartmouth. There she took the fancy of Mr and Mrs E. P. Cheston of Warsash, Hants. They were members of the Newhaven & Seaford Sailing Club and had the boat at Fairey Marine on the Hamble. Taking advantage of the radar, the echo-sounding equipment and the host of electronic conveniences installed by the Osbornes, they intended to take *Bluefinch* and live on her in the Mediterranean. What happened to this plan I do not know, for the Chestons eventually went to live in Spain without the boat. Within a few months of purchase from the Osbornes, Len Cox of Cox & Haswell Ltd. at Poole was surveying her for her next owners who reinstated her original name.

Yet more of the *Blue Bird* coincidences, waiting in the wings for a number of years, were about to occur. When Ron Blindell was coming to the end of his ownership in

1963 he employed a secretary named Audrey Thompson. Her father-in-law had been at school with Malcolm Campbell whose son Donald went to school with Audrey's husband Richard. Imagine her surprise when, eleven years later, Richard announced that he had found a motor yacht called *Bluefinch*. She was for sale on a pontoon opposite the Sun Inn at Warsash, and he planned to buy her.

The Thompsons had their first boat in 1948. It was a small, cramped motor yacht on the Thames in which Audrey tried to provide out of her ration books for the friends and acquaintances who popped in to admire the ship. At one time they lived on a Thames sailing barge. By 1974 Richard was the Director of a firm of agricultural merchants. *Bluefinch* was to be owned by them in partnership with Donald Saunders, the husband of Audrey's sister Beryl. This same partnership also had business interests in a holiday development in Sardinia. They intended to use *Bluefinch* to ferry holidaymakers around nearby coastal waters.

In May 1974 they negotiated a selling price of £11,750 and *Bluefinch* spent six weeks on the hard at Fairey Marine being refurbished. Richard Thompson discovered that the name *Blue Bird* had become vacant following Donald Campbell's death on Coniston Water in 1967. He set in train the formalities needed to reinstate *Blue Bird*'s original name, advertising his intentions in the *Falmouth Packet*, the *Camborne Redruth Packet* and the *Helston Packet*. It took six months to complete; *Blue Bird* appeared as one word on the documents but on the boat it was written as two. The new owners also added their own blue bird to the bows; unlike the chubby little chap of Campbell's day, this one had the unmistakable lines of a swallow.

For most of the next two years *Blue Bird* was kept in the canal basin at Exeter, Devon. There was just the one

The new bluebird motif

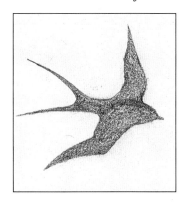

Blue Bird *in the mid 1970s*

abortive attempt to take her to Sardinia. *Blue Bird* slipped quietly out of Dartmouth at 11.00 p.m. on a calm, clear night at the end of May 1975. She was bound for Le Havre and had on board all the owners, some family and friends. On her stern davits she carried a newly-designed, two-man jet boat which was to be tested in the shallow waters of Sardinia. By 3 o'clock in the morning all hell was let loose. *Blue Bird* was in a Force 7, with fog and driving rain. The jet boat was breaking loose from the davits. People were being ill, and her progress was in the hands of a novice with strict instructions to watch the controls, report if anything looked wrong, but do nothing else.

Suddenly the engine compartment flooded with oil and one engine seized up. The crankshaft was damaged, and the automatic pilot packed up. Out of the darkness loomed a huge oil tanker. As it went by *Blue Bird* called urgently on the radio; the response was in Japanese and the tanker carried on.

Down below a door slammed shut in one of the watertight bulkheads, effectively entombing Audrey for the next ten hours. The for'ard hatch, which might have been her only means of escape, was securely bolted on the outside. The boat pitched and rolled; everything moveable fell and crashed about the cabin. Through the portlights she saw alternately sky and water as *Blue Bird* lunged about, and she feared that every time the boat went down it would not come back up again.

When land was sighted, it turned out to be Cherbourg, where *Blue Bird* spent two weeks under repair. It took another three weeks to get her down the canals to

72

Lyon and she damaged her propeller on debris in the water. By now the original crew had almost all left the boat of necessity, and the voyage was finally abandoned at the Yacht Club du Rhone at St. Germain de Mont d'Or. *Blue Bird* was repaired and brought back to Devon.

Blue Bird *in distress while crossing the Channel, May 1975*

Meanwhile a Doncaster engineer had been on the lookout for a traditional boat. T. R. Bingham owned a company which made cutting instruments for the coal industry. On holiday in Devon with his wife, a chance advertisement caught his eye. The yacht broker took the Binghams to Exeter canal where *Blue Bird* was moored, and she proved to be just what they wanted. Negotiations completed, the Binghams took possession and set off against the cross currents in Exeter harbour. The engines stalled. Faced with having to stop very quickly or hit the lock gates, they bumped into a pier at 8 knots. It could have been disaster, but in the event there was damage to the bow which had to be fixed straight away. Hardly the maiden voyage under their ownership for which the Binghams would have wished.

Blue Bird was taken back to the Hamble at Southampton where she was enjoyed by the whole family - often nine strong - on holidays in the coastal waters of southern England. When their eldest daughter took up horse riding back in Yorkshire the visits to the Hamble gradually became less frequent.

When *Motor Boat & Yachting* magazine included a piece about *Blue Bird* in 1980 they mentioned that she was for sale. In due course Terry Bingham received a letter simply addressed "Mr & Mrs T. R. Bingham, Blue Bird, Yorkshire." How on earth they managed to deliver that to the correct address in Doncaster, only the Post Office knows!

The result of this was that *Blue Bird* went to Bill Finnerty, an American then living in Brussels where he ran a restaurant. Mr Finnerty paid over £17,000 in cash, handed over to Terry Bingham in a suitcase at Southampton. Terry then spent half the night trying to find a hotel which would let him put the money in their safe!

Garrick Bingham, the owner's brother, took *Blue Bird* from the Hamble to Dover and then to Ostend where Bill Finnerty was waiting to take delivery. A year or so later she was back at Fairey Marine, where former owner Donald Saunders came across her looking much the worse for wear. He was told she had been used as a houseboat in Finnerty's absence by hippy squatters and needed to be refurbished.

In fact under Finnerty's ownership *Blue Bird* had at least two years of cruising in the Mediterranean; he chartered her as well as living on board with his wife, and the boat was frequently around the ports of Spain, Majorca, Ibiza and the Balearic Islands.

ACT FIVE

Restoration

"... I am the joy of seeing what is beautiful, who have loved you so dearly. We are very happy but we cannot see beyond our dreams..."

Maeterlinck, *The Blue Bird*

Bluebird of Chelsea, *fully
restored and more beautiful
than ever before*

When Tara asked the ingenuous question "Why don't *we* have a boat, daddy"? back in 1984, it was certainly well timed. That summer I had rented a house in Sardinia and with it a Riva speedboat moored right in the harbour. I needed someone to teach me how to drive it. So I invited Scott Beadle to join the family for a few days and "show me the ropes", so to speak. He and I had worked closely on a photographic flip-book project of mine about Ailsa Craig and besides being an art school teacher, set designer and art director, he seemed to have an encyclopaedic knowledge of boats and the etiquette and technical names that go with them.

The Riva speedboat

To have a Riva speedboat moored close by was a joy, but the shallowest part of the harbour where it lay was full of invisible rope and debris which invariably fouled our propellers. Snorkelling in a murky harbour is not to be recommended but we shared the daily burden and laughed. In the end Scott stayed until the end of the holiday and I discovered the thrill of being at the helm of my own boat - even if it was a rented one.

Back in London, three months later, provoked by Tara's question, I suggested to Scott that we should look out for some sort of old boat to keep at Cadogan Pier. His eyes lit up and by the end of the week, having combed the yachting magazines, he had come up with six possibilities. "One is a cut above the rest". he said "see if you can tell which". It was not difficult. There in the November issue of *Yachting World* was a photograph in a small advertisement which seemed to leap out at me - *Bluebird II built for Sir Malcolm Campbell in 1931 by Thornycroft of Hampton Wick. 51' x 11'.6" x 5'.6". Mahogany on oak. Twin Perkins 6.354.*

The island of Ailsa Craig

77

"BLUEBIRD II" built for SIR MALCOLM CAMPBELL in 1931 by THORNYCROFT of HAMPTON WICK. 51' x 11' 6" x 5' 6". Mah on oak. Twin Perkins 6.354. Beautiful yacht for living on; capable of passing thro' the French Canals. Med. £25,000.

The advertisement in
Yachting World

Beautiful yacht for living on, capable of passing thro' the French Canals. Little did I know that the photograph was taken in her heyday.

When Bill Finnerty came to sell *Blue Bird* in 1984, he contacted Philip Bristow, then a yacht broker at his Stone Pier Yard, to do the job for him. "It was a commission right out of the blue", Bristow told me, "the sort brokers get from time to time. I never saw Mr Finnerty. We communicated by letter and telephone wherever he happened to be at the time and I think his final payment was made into a bank in America". The boat itself was lying at J. Bjorg's yard, Grau du Roi in the South of France. The asking price was an optimistic £25,000. Otherwise Mr Finnerty was of a mind to take her up through France and try to sell her in Belgium the following year. I say 'optimistic' with hindsight, of course; in my initial naivety I had thought it to be a reasonable amount for such a piece of history.

This was the moment when Scott saw the advertisement. We were already in a hurry. But luckily the broker, Philip Bristow, had listed an after hours number. "Yes, she is still for sale. But no, I have not had an opportunity to see her" he reported. "But I do know of a certain Len Cox who I believe surveyed her more than once in the sixties". When I spoke to Len Cox he said that he had not seen her for nearly twenty years, but he reminisced fondly and promised to send me a photograph of her taken in the '30s. This single photograph was to sustain me through the months of negotiation and the dark days of restoration. If she had once looked like that, I thought, she could again.

78

Down in the Camargue, Bjorg was overhauling the engines. From his office in the United States, Bill Finnerty assured everyone that once this was done she would be in good enough condition to make a voyage through France and across the Channel. "The decks look a bit tatty", he informed Philip Bristow, "but the hull is sound and the strength is there". This was reassuring news, and if it proved to be true I would have a piece of history at a reasonable price. Scott would know; he was an experienced sailor who had once helped build a 33' cutter in Mexico.

Two weeks later, Scott and I flew to Marseilles to meet the American owner in Grau du Roi in the Camargue. From the beginning, things began to go wrong. Just outside Arles, we chanced upon the exact same viewpoint from which Van Gogh had painted one of his famous landscapes. I had seen it at the great exhibition of his work at the Metropolitan Museum in New York six months previously. On returning to the hire car, we found that the engine would not start. Impatient and frustrated, we eventually got

First sight of **Blue Bird** *at Grau du Roi*

79

it going and roared off in search of the elusive *Blue Bird*.

On entering Grau du Roi, the road follows alongside the canal. Turning a corner, suddenly there she was. It took just one glimpse, even with - or perhaps because of - my layman's eyes, to realise that we were going to be bitterly disappointed. I looked at Scott for some sign that he might instantly have recognised some potential that had escaped me, but in his eyes I saw only a reflection of my own feelings. The boat was decrepit and sad. We looked at each other and shrugged our shoulders. A loss to be written off to experience, I thought. But fate decreed otherwise. We stared in amazement as at first glance she looked the same, but somehow something was different. We sat and compared the original photograph with what we saw. The mast had been re-positioned on the aft deck, the wheelhouse had been raked and a flying bridge added over the original sliding sunshine roof, and that sharp elegance with which I was already familiar from Len Cox's photograph was now spoilt.

We parked and crossed the bridge over the canal to where Bill Finnerty was patiently waiting for us. Once on board, it did not take us more than a few minutes to realise that this had been a wild goose chase. Sadly, Finnerty's wife had died two years previously and he had returned to the United States. Hence *Blue Bird*'s neglect. She was rotten and there was spongy, crumbling woodwork everywhere. Rotting fabric and Formica with Heath Robinson wiring abounded.

Miraculously, Finnerty coaxed the starboard engine to life but apologised for the other one which was temporarily out of order. Out in the bay in a long swell we rolled and lurched and I began to feel distinctly queasy. Somehow, I couldn't seem to catch Scott's eye, but for me it was a simple decision and the sooner we ended this performance the better.

80

We returned to the mooring and repaired to the local cafe, where I intended to say, as politely as possible, "Thank you, but no". Briefly I went to the car and to my consternation realised that it had been broken into. Gone were our suitcases, cameras, money; in fact everything. This was a major blow and having reported the loss to the police, it took me quite a few coffees and Armagnacs to simmer down. Poor Bill Finnerty, who had come from Holland just to see us, saw any possible hope of a sale evaporating before his very eyes. He begged us not to make any decision until we had again been out on *Blue Bird* the following morning and please would we not stay in the same God-forsaken hotel, but return to Aigues Mortes, 15 kms away, where at least we could find a decent meal and clean rooms.

These we found and the 'patron' promised to cook us a meal to remember. This was just as well as we had much to forget. Hopes dashed, dreams unfulfilled, disillusion and gloom. However, the meal was good as was the wine and at midnight - thoroughly fortified - we decided for old times' sake to drive back and take one last look. The road seemed longer than 15 kms this time, but eventually we parked the car in a convenient place from where we could floodlight the boat with the car's yellow headlights. Access was no problem, as *Blue Bird* was unlocked, and we went aboard. Sensibly I had brought with me two glasses and the remains of the bottle of Armagnac from the restaurant and we installed ourselves in the saloon. In the quietness of the night, stage-lit through the portholes by the headlights, her true character began to re-emerge and a dialogue began. As we explored from stem to stern, we found that her interior had suffered less than her exterior. Here were mahogany bunks and wardrobes, there an original cupboard and everywhere the evocative feeling of a bye-gone era.

Two hours later, not knowing what to think, we

returned to the car, only to find that its battery was exhausted and so were we. It was December, bitterly cold with the beginnings of snow, and neither of us relished the walk home. The nearby main road was virtually deserted and anyway, would you risk stopping in a remote French village to pick up two disreputable looking characters at 3.00 a.m. in the morning? One lady nearly did but on realising that there were two of us, sped away in alarm.

When in doubt, go to the police. They would remember us from our morning visit, I felt, but would they respond to our incessant pealing on the bell? No. Eventually when we had rattled his window with enough gravel, a sleepy but irate gendarme appeared. After much explanation and desperate references to the *Entente Cordiale*, he reluctantly called us a taxi which duly arrived within the hour. He deposited us at our hotel and promised to return at 8.00 a.m. with a set of jump leads, which I had described in mime.

The following morning, fate stepped in. They don't seem to like 'plastic money' in Aigues Mortes. "Je regrette, monsieur, le cheque ou cash mais pas la carte de credit, vous comprenez". I was dismayed, but undeterred we left our bags, promising to return at noon to settle up. We drove to Grau du Roi to meet Bill Finnerty who, I by now realised, could be my only hope of obtaining sufficient funds to pay the hotel bill. I didn't actually agree there and then to buy *Blue Bird*, but he did at least risk making me a loan.

Returning to London, we tried to think rationally and sensibly. If she was worth restoring, we would have to send a competent surveyor to assess the implications. My insurance agent, Gilbert Dix, recommended an experienced man named Frank Payne who came to London one day to see us. He is a splendid fellow, a lover of wooden boats and he immediately picked up on the romance of restoring a famous Dunkirk Little Ship as we now knew her to be. He became infused with our enthusiasm and promised within a few weeks to go down to see her and make a sober report.

The wait seemed interminable and we searched endlessly for alternatives but it soon became apparent that it was to be *Blue Bird* or nothing. I sent the money back to Bill Finnerty and alerted him of Frank Payne's imminent visit. With trepidation, when the survey finally arrived, I flicked through the first few pages and read his last paragraph. The bottom line said that she had been built well and that the hull was still sound, but little else. If we were prepared to take a deep breath, she still could be saved.

It doesn't take much imagination to appreciate her true condition when you know that, after some negotiation, I payed less than £15,000 for her; but now she was mine and I was over the moon. At Frank's suggestion we contacted a delivery skipper called Ginge Sergeant whose exploits I had recently read about. During a storm in the Bermuda Triangle while delivering a yacht, he was washed overboard but managed to clamber back and deliver the yacht to her owner without fuss at the appointed hour. This seemed to be the right sort of man for our job and so Ginge was dispatched with adequate funds and a mate to attempt the return journey through the canals of France.

Homeward bound, in a lock somewhere in France

Intermittent reports came back that the port engine was beyond repair but the starboard one, although precarious, was up and running properly. He was advised to take a tow from a barge as far as Lyon as the experts said she would never make it on one engine against the strong current of the River Rhone. So, on 3rd March, with much head shaking from the locals, *Blue Bird* commenced the long haul home. She had been

83

lying at her mooring for nearly three years, undisturbed and like many a great old lady, prepared to let the world go by and fade into obscurity watching the Mediterranean. I had at some moments speculated that maybe the reason so many things had gone wrong was that she was an unlucky boat, but deep down I was sure she was really only testing our fortitude for what lay ahead. Don't forget, she hadn't been built by a pessimist.

As news came through, Scott and I plotted her painfully slow progress as Ginge was apparently having one problem after another. But he's not a quitter and eventually we made a plan to rendezvous near Dijon the next weekend. When we finally met up, *Blue Bird* had taken on a new lease of life. Her decks had been scrubbed and her metal work polished. There were even flowers on the table. Despite the drips from the leaking deck at night, we thoroughly enjoyed the next few days. On one occasion, returning from re-victualling at the local store, we passed a 'still' farm from which emanated the most tantalising aroma of warm fruity alcohol. We entered the darkened rooms and were treated to a sample of the finest Mirabel I have ever tasted. Sadly we were not allowed to buy any but when we offered a bottle of 'The Famous Grouse' in exchange, they filled up an empty champagne bottle with their delectable ambrosia and presented it to us. Back on board, Ginge misguidedly took this to be flat champagne and I'm afraid he missed an excellent dinner that night.

Another day we had our first female company. A stunning model from St. Laurent, whom I had met, braved the journey to join us for lunch. She was not overly impressed with damp boats and said she preferred nice hotels. Would I by any chance be in Paris next Saturday night? Eagerly Scott and I worked out the distance and replied "Yes, if nothing goes wrong, there is just a chance that we could be". It did. One morning, for no apparent reason, the rudder broke and almost before we knew what was happening we had turned broadside, touching the banks at either end, in the path of an oncoming, unstoppable barge. We leapt ashore, and it was only with superhuman strength that we managed to pull her bows round in time, so that the barge missed her by inches. Otherwise she would have been reduced to

Broadside, and in danger of a collision

matchwood. Ginge and Scott repaired the rudder with, of all things, a bent spoon and though she leaked and she listed we made up time and arrived in Paris on the Saturday at 5.00 p.m.

I had booked a romantic room at the Ritz and my lady friend had agreed to meet me at 8.45 p.m. On arrival, I bathed, put on my best Noel Coward dressing gown, opened a bottle of champagne and summoned the chef. The Ritz is the epitome of discretion and the reservations manager, my friend David Campbell, knowing presumably from the chef that I was entertaining, telephoned me with a

Blue Bird *on the Seine*

85

suggestion. As there was to be a reception with many photographers in the foyer that evening, maybe the young lady would prefer to come to the Rue Cambon entrance from where she could be escorted up the back stairs to my room.

These instructions were duly passed on, but at 8.45 p.m. disaster struck. St. Laurent at the last moment had ordered one more fashion showing and she would not be able to come at all. Bitterly disappointed, when Scott rang to see how things were going I told him the news and suggested he came and share the exquisite meal I had ordered. Without thinking, I told him to come to the Rue Cambon entrance. When he arrived he was unshaven but wearing a particularly jaunty Breton sailor's top. I don't think my reputation has ever been the same since. Scott says that as he left, he was unceremoniously booted out of the back door. Ah well!

After a few days of well-deserved rest, we decided to give a lunch on board. We raided Fauchon and in the company of Isabel Goldsmith and Coco Brown, had a sumptuous picnic cruising up and down the Seine passing Notre Dame. Easter Sunday found us in Rouen where I left *Blue Bird* to her crew for the trip to Le Havre.

There the weather was bad and they had to wait for a suitable opportunity but on 8th April, 182 locks and 36 eventful days after leaving the Camargue, they braved the elements and attempted to cross the Channel. All seemed to be going well until, within sight of land, the starboard engine decided it had had enough and gave up the ghost.

Without power the boat would just have drifted at the mercy of the tide. Ginge got the radio working and an urgency call brought the Selsey Bill lifeboat *City of London* which stood by and checked the drift whilst *Blue Bird*'s crew tried to restart the engine. But the fuel was too badly contaminated and a tow was gratefully accepted into Portsmouth harbour. Next day a beer barrel of fresh fuel was rigged up in the wheelhouse and gravity fed to the engine which immediately started up. In this way they reached Poole which was to be *Blue Bird's* home for the next twelve months.

Once again at Frank Payne's suggestion, we had been in touch with a firm of highly skilled shipwrights called H & T Marine at Mitchell's Boatyard. They were waiting for *Blue Bird* with anticipation and some trepidation.

H & T Marine is a boatbuilding firm with an impressive pedigree who are equally at home with wood and glass fibre. The partnership was formed in 1975 when shipwright Bernard Hiscock teamed up with Graham Titterington, a master joiner. Bernard, and Teddy Martin who was to go with him, had been with Randall & McGregor, in their day perhaps the best wooden boat builders on the south coast. They in their turn had come out of R. A. Newman, the well-known, old-established shipbuilder with a reputation second to none. The men of H & T Marine have been associated with projects as diverse as the Trade Wind 33 class yachts and the Geddes family's clinker-built harbour launch. So it was with complete confidence that I entrusted them with the rebuilding of *Blue Bird*, and they were to prove every bit as good as their recommendation.

The original intention was to bring *Blue Bird* ashore at the Royal Motor Yacht Club, Poole. But having done away with their slipway the RMYC had only a hoist capable of lifting fifteen tons, thereby imposing a limit on the size of boats allowed into the yard. If this could have been overcome in essence, H & T intended to get the boat out of the water with a wheel cradle and a 25-ton crane. Eventually she was put ashore at the Poole Harbour Yacht Club and

In Poole harbour, April 1985

Blue Bird *with scaffolding, ready for work to begin*

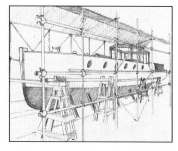

87

Debris collects on the deck as work begins

Brian Kimber's clock, made from the original propeller shafts of **Blue Bird**

brought into Saltern's Boatyard on a hoist frequently used by BBC television in making the *Howard's Way* series. Saltern's had been contracted to see to the mechanics and the electrics in the charge of Brian Kimber - the foreman engineer and latterly yard manager. Brian was an electro-mechanical engineer by trade, so he took on the electrical side. His colleague Mike Wills saw to the mechanics.

"I never thought she would float again", was Brian's initial reaction. "We had to rebuild the two Perkins diesel engines. In fact one of them wasn't a marine engine at all, but had been put together from some commercial application. They both had a different power output, so that had to be sorted out as well. Then she needed a new propeller shaft, remote controls, steering gear and electrical equipment. There's literally miles of wire and trunking on the boat now".

This side of the project was to take six months. Of course Saltern's took off *Blue Bird's* original bronze propeller shafts, now defunct, but which had powered the boat when she went to Dunkirk. Brian, a clock maker in his spare time, used the material from the propeller shafts to make one of his clocks.

Ever since we had bought *Blue Bird* Scott and I had been discussing how to restore her, but in the initial stages it was difficult to know where to begin as there was so much to do. Whilst she was gradually taken to pieces, we began to realise that the whole project was very much bigger than it had at first seemed, and I must admit that the original ideas bear little resemblance to the way she looks now. Ideas would bubble up, develop, be

88

reconsidered and sometimes discarded but always taken seriously. Scott somehow knew what I was striving for and how much of a perfectionist I am and managed to take my, in many cases, impractical ideas, interpret them and convey them to the team at H & T and make them work. Any early quotations soon went by the board as I realised that to do it properly no corners could be cut. Also for Teddy

The saloon with all fixtures and fittings removed

Martin, the master craftsman who was about to retire, this was an opportunity for him to demonstrate his supreme boat building skills.

And so it was to be. By the time everything was stripped out, *Blue Bird* comprised just a keel, ribs and the hull sides. Only by the most careful placing of a number of shores, beams and stretchers could she be persuaded to keep

The saloon fully restored and refitted

her long, slim hull in shape. We surveyed the ever-increasing pile of rotting wood, ancient machinery and general debris and found some quite salvageable gems. Amongst the original furniture all the bunk facings and locker drawers were saved, as were the saloon cabinets and Campbell's writing desk. Most of the deck beams, both wheels and the mast and tabernacle had survived in good

89

The new deck half laid

The new deck completed

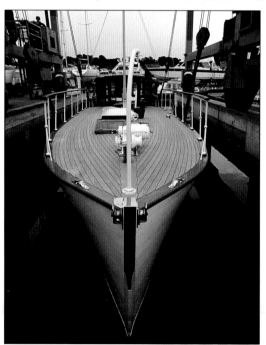

condition, and much deck furniture was original and restorable. Bernard and Graham smiled and shrugged their shoulders: "Aye, she's a fine boat Mr Summers; bit more work than expected, but she'll be well worth it".

Scott was beginning to feel increasingly guilty. He felt he had coaxed and cajoled me and sworn undying loyalty just as long as I bought the boat, and here was *Blue Bird* turning into a monstrous dinghy. An ever-increasing number of council skips seemed to be taking her away. Of course I had really needed no encouragement after the initial hiccup at Grau du Roi, but Scott felt responsible. He couldn't get it out of his mind that all I had originally asked for was "a small 20' - 25' runabout suitable for the river".

When we surveyed some of the pictures of *Blue Bird* taken in the early '30s, we quickly realised that some seemingly small but very important modifications had been made. These seriously altered the period feel of the boat. Probably the most notable were the raked windows at the for'ard end of the wheelhouse and the large overhanging eyebrow above. These combined to give much more of a late '40s or early '50s look. Additionally, the loss of the original sunshine roof, replaced with a fixed perspex skylight surmounted by an external screen, helped to make the decision to scrap the whole wheelhouse (rot had been discovered as well) much more bearable.

An inspection of the decks revealed serious deterioration. Although she originally

90

had canvas-covered ply decks, this was one feature we decided to modify. We felt that her long foredeck leant itself to curved runs of laid teak. Tony Harding prepared a tongue-and-grooved pine underdeck, sealed with a membrane of glass, cloth and epoxy. (Over this was laid the teak deck glued and pinned to its deckbeams.) It was beautifully done and has given us already four years of virtually leak proof living under some quite harsh conditions. Whilst the decks were off and the wheelhouse removed, Brian Kimber and his team of engineers removed the engines, gearboxes, old wiring, shafts, skin fittings, tanks etc., for inspection.

We decided to rebuild the 1967 engines from the bottom up. To make *Blue Bird* a completely comfortable cruising yacht of the late 1980s, Brian was now required to find space for much more equipment in the engine room. This had been quite adequate in the '30's when she was fitted with 4-cylinder Thornycroft petrol engines and a small half-kilowatt generator. But it was going to prove

Graham Parker in the engine room

extremely tight with a pair of 6-cylinder diesels, a 10kVA generator in its own soundproofed housing, mounted thwartships, two fifteen gallon calorifiers, a large pressure water pump, two Eberspacher heaters, a constavolt and at that time twelve 12-volt batteries. It is to Brian's everlasting credit that not only did he achieve this and more, but in fact it is really quite cosy down there, and by no means a difficult installation to work on.

During this time the design team had been joined by Graham

The Aston Martin/Lagonda

Parker, who was to take responsibility for the lighting design and to liaise with Brian on most things electrical. I had got to know him well when he worked extensively on my house. We all felt that other than traditional bulkhead lights, most yacht light fittings seemed rather limited and cheap. I had some very simple, but elegant brass picture lights which Graham and Brian modified to 24v. These along with small halogen spotlights in the galley, heads and bathroom, together with bulkhead lights in corridors and companionways completed the lighting rig.

Graham, who had no previous nautical experience, has, like the rest of us, become completely captivated by *Blue Bird*. He is now a tried and trusted crewman, with over 6,000 cruising miles under his belt, besides becoming a great friend.

We were all now well hooked. Every weekend we prepared a picnic hamper, with a few beers, and drove down to Poole in my Aston Martin/Lagonda, itself an historic vehicle, being one of only six built. Everyone always looked forward to these journeys. Much work would be done, decisions made and usually sketches and drawings would take shape during lunch in the Antelope pub in Poole. On one such occasion the whole galley was designed on the back of an envelope. It proved an extremely durable design, and if you compare it with the galley as it is now, you can see there's virtually no difference. Scott's ability to sketch accurately made everybody's life much easier.

While the hull was bare, Teddy Martin carried out a close inspection of the planking and frames. Wherever required, any cracked ribs were doubled using a full length of similar size, steamed in behind both the beam shelf and stringers. The doublers were all through-riveted with copper fastenings. Although all the hull planking was cleaned back to bare timber and found to be in excellent condition, there was evidence of poor earlier repair work. This was replaced

The rebuilt hatch

92

together with some short lengths of planking at the break in the shear, but the real problem was found in the transom. There was considerable long-term damage and rot where the transom and hull joined. It was decided to cut six inches off the hull planking and fit a new mahogany transom, thus saving considerable cost in stripping all the hull planks back. Interestingly, when the boat was re-measured by Bureau Veritas, it was found still to be exactly 52' long.

Tom Brown and Geoffrey Collins restoring the aft cabin

Throughout the period of dismantling, a picture and a feeling had emerged of how the style of the boat should develop. There were certain original features such as stop-chamfered panelling which could be extended throughout the rebuilt and redesigned portions, to conform to the period. Formica had been used to cover the bulkheads, but when this was removed it was found to conceal tongue-and-groove mahogany. The mahogany was mutilated by poor wiring, but gave us an idea of how it originally was, so it was only a question of replacing all bulkheads with new timbers. Peg-board had found a place in the saloon as a liner between the portlights. Although in this case there was no knowing what had been there in the '30s it wasn't difficult to realise that mahogany panels would perfectly match other parts of the boat.

All the while, rough drawings and sketches enabled us to convey some of our ideas to the shipwrights. These helped overcome some of the inevitable misunderstandings caused by their use of rather specialised language, and sometimes our lack of it. For instance I was still wondering why they all sounded so worried about lowering the mast easily for the bridges during spring tides. After all, if these happened only once a year I was sure we would manage!

Around this time we were joined by other workers. One of them, named Tom Brown, was to continue working on *Blue Bird* at Cadogan Pier in London for some considerable time, finishing off many of our late requirements. Tom became very much a part of our team and it was a great pleasure to work with him.

The A-bracket bearing the shafts and props had been removed, but Teddy found it was not possible to re-align the stern tubes so the A-brackets themselves were modified, refastened and re-aligned. The shafts were of phosphor-bronze and badly worn, so we replaced them with stainless steel ones. A nice touch, typical of the thought put into their work, was Teddy's idea to turn the main compass supports from a section of the old shafts.

Much of the work on *Blue Bird* was of course from structural necessity or an unavoidable engineering requirement. For example, no one would argue that a power boat needs engines in excellent condition. Consequently many decisions were taken by the yard as to what constituted a safe and secure boat. Our specification for the design and equipment was really based on the future use of the boat balanced with the style of the '30s. At the same time we wanted to take advantage of modern materials so that the boat would be both practical and comfortable by today's standards.

The galley was rather small, the boat quite narrow and the turn of the bilge seriously interfered, for example, with fitting any standard box-shaped cookers or fridges. We

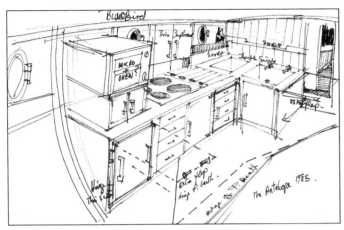

(above) Scott's original design for the galley, sketched on the back of an envelope at the Antelope pub, Poole, in May 1985

The galley looking aft (above) and (left) the view towards the saloon

95

decided to hand build the 24-volt fridge to the shape of the hull side, thus maximising its capacity. At the same time we decided there was no good space for a normal domestic cooker, so we fitted a four-ring hob and a combined microwave and conventional oven at eye level. The work surface ran the full length of the galley with drop flaps at either end to create extra space. We chose a very hard-wearing, heat resistant moulded material called Corian which was beautiful and has proved incredibly durable. All the shelves and cupboards are stop chamfered mahogany panels similar to the rest of the boat. We decided that the galley should be all-electric. This was partly because the boat spends almost all the year away from marinas and Scott knew it would inevitably be used by people without any particular boat experience and he feared potential trouble with gas. He would worry whether it was all switched off properly when he wasn't there. To avoid using the generator we keep a small calor gas stove to make tea or coffee when we are in a marina and need to retain the goodwill of our neighbours. The design of the galley has proved perfect for a boat that spends nearly all its time in rivers and canals, and also on long sea trips. We are never at sea for much more than twenty-four hours so there is actually no need for a gimballed stove.

Work progressed quite well throughout the boat and soon it was time to install our rebuilt Perkins engines. This was made much easier because at that point we had no wheelhouse at all. We also fitted an H.F.L. 10 kVA 3-cylinder generator mounted thwartships over the port shaft. This was a very snug fit in its own soundproof box, but again was accessible from every side, including aft where access was gained by removing a tongue-and-grooved panel in the bathroom. The calorifiers fitted for'ard on the outside of each engine were of a combined 30 gallons

The first rough idea of what the bathroom might look like

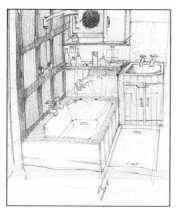

96

The varnished mahogany bath, inlaid with ash

capacity, enough for some piping hot showers, or more particularly for two very hot deep baths.

We kept the bathroom immediately for'ard of the owner's cabin. What it was like in Campbell's day I can only imagine, but my inspiration for a wooden bath came from the 1936 John Alden designed *Royona*, featured in *Classic Yacht Interiors*. *Royona* was fitted out with a beautiful octagonal mahogany sink; on *Blue Bird* this was to become a bath using ash for the inlay. "If varnish can keep water out", I remember saying to Bernard Hiscock, "then it can

The wheelhouse instrument panel under construction (above) and (right) the completed wheelhouse

(Above) wheels dismantled for varnishing

(Right) the wheelhouse looking aft

keep water in". -"It's made like a dinghy inside out", said Bernard, more practically. The result is a most beautiful bath which, although constantly used, has neither leaked nor needed revarnishing.

Original photographs, taken at the time of *Blue Bird's* trials in 1931 were used to work out the shape of the wheelhouse. During the rebuilding in the mid-1960s its shape had been changed and new materials, unknown in Malcolm Campbell's time, had been introduced. I was anxious to go back to the original wherever possible. We wanted to restore the big sunshine roof to provide fresh air on sunny days and allow good contact between the interior and the outside steering position. Making the aft windows open enabled us to pass up food to the outside dining area. In front we broke with the original design by putting in a single window instead of a split one. We had 15 mm Lexon storm screens made for this and for the wheelhouse side lights. The wonderful visibility you get from the wide windscreen is fine on the river, but in the open seas, we needed the storm screens more than once particularly rounding Ardnamurchan Point in a Force 6/7.

Inside the wheelhouse we designed the primary and secondary instrument layouts to be as elegant and unobtrusive as possible, as they are all modern instruments. The Decca, Nakamichi tape deck, VHF, Halon and generator controls are mounted in their own console between the aft windows. All engine controls, log, echo sounder, switches and tank gauges are positioned immediately in front of the helmsman and the whole layout is dominated by a beautiful 1937 Brass Admiralty Pattern Compass. To port is a folding navigation table and locker for navigation instruments. A bench seat, housing a dehumidifier and stowage to port, and a seat with wine storage to starboard completed our wheelhouse layout.

The table laid on the aft deck

The after deck had previously been redesigned to accommodate seating instead of the dinghy, and we decided to keep this arrangement and include a permanently fitted dining table. It is this all-weather capability that has made *Blue Bird* so enjoyable. If it is wet and dreary then we have dinner or drinks below in the warmth of the saloon. On fine days we eat outside on the 'poop deck'.

I imagine that all owners of historical boats share a fascination for their vessels' history and the artefacts which were part of it. In rebuilding so much of *Blue Bird* we still retained everything we could which was original and have gathered items associated with the boat's history as well as her illustrious first owner. I should like to have obtained some of Malcolm Campbell's original and distinctive Blue

Bird table ware but when this was not to be, commissioned my own Limoges service.

Accommodation on *Blue Bird* is arranged in three cabins: a V-berth, a Pilot berth with upper and lower bunks, and the owner's aft cabin with a double bunk. All of the accommodation forward including the for'ard head is finished in slatted mahogany. This is probably one of the most traditional and practical ways of allowing free movement of air around the hull, and looks superb. Looking now at Thornycroft's original drawings (alas not found in 1985) we noticed that the owner's aft cabin was actually divided into two separate cabins. They must have been extremely cramped little berths, and our present large single cabin is a much better arrangement.

It was in this cabin that I felt I wanted to change the conventional idea of a sea berth, and create a cabin with a unique style. I talked to Scott's fiancee Gaynor Hill, a soft-furnishings designer, about a birthday card she sent me made of various velvets and chintzes. One in particular had caught my eye: a ribbon and rose chintz by Warner. Gaynor had the carpenters make up the panels which she then padded and fitted to the combings and forward bulkhead.

Bluebird of Chelsea's
Limoges dinner service

The V-berth cabin

101

The master cabin under construction

The rest of this fabric was used to make a matching bedspread. The seat and occasional berth opposite was upholstered in ruby-red velvet and the bolsters were in matching chenille. There are two hanging lockers aft with a dressing table and drawers between. Comfortable as the double berth was, I found that there was not quite enough leg room so I divided the hanging locker with a 'stable' door so that the bottom half folds flat, thus giving about two extra feet of leg room. Above the dressing table the whole aft bulkhead is covered with mirror which has the portlight cut into it. This is practical and helps to create the illusion of more space. The Nakamichi stereo sound system is mounted above the bed with the speakers concealed in the locker doors. There is a telephone on the opposite side of the bed which completes the facilities. The result is a unique master cabin which is practical as a sea berth and which gets close to my desire to be as un-nautical as possible, and creates the feel of a Tissot painting.

The matching fabrics and wall-coverings

Blue Bird was rapidly nearing completion now. Gaynor and Christine Fownes, our upholsterer, had taken all the fabrics for the rest of the boat to her studio in London. We had decided to standardise the colour and type of fabric throughout except for the main saloon seating and the master cabin. All upholstery inside and out was to be a green cord with red

102

A view of the master cabin with the original dressing table

piping, and matching green carpets. Cord is a good material to use on a well-heated boat, and wears well to give a more comfortable appearance than when new. Now it only remained for Gaynor to stitch together the Peruvian mantas and have them fitted.

The purchase of the Peruvian wool mantas is an example of the lengths to which I was prepared to go in restoring *Blue Bird*. The fabric came from Chinceros, a small village centred on its mission church, remotely situated at about 11,000 feet above sea level in the high Andes. I had previously been there during the 1970s and bought some of the very hard-wearing, weather-beaten cloth which the Indians make out of llama wool or alpaca. Vegetable dyes give the material its vibrant colours and this is made into

Sunday market, Chinceros, Peru

103

Scott's original interpretation of our ideas for the saloon

totally authentic mantas or shawls. I well remembered how well this had stood up to its use on a sofa over the years, and thought it would be just the thing for *Blue Bird's* saloon. I was in Los Angeles at the beginning of a weekend and took the decision to fly down to Peru and visit the Sunday market at Chineros. By Monday I was back again with the material I had chosen.

Now this would make the perfect finishing touch to complement the richness of the mahogany in the saloon. With cushions and bolsters in the same fabric, the whole effect is one of exotic places, nicely finished off with Persian rugs on the cabin floor. All the old cabin furnishings had been restored and put back in their place, and with her

The gleaming mahogany is the ideal foil for the richly coloured Peruvian fabrics

104

white deckheads and varnished oak beams, she truly looked a picture.

When stepping on board for the first time one is immediately struck by the sheer quality finish of the paint and varnish. In Geoffrey Collins we had an absolute perfectionist. There are twelve coats of varnish inside, each one rubbed down to give a glass-like finish, and the paint is more like lacquer.

It was a beautiful spring morning, 19th April 1986, when *Blue Bird* emerged from her shed and was carried in the mechanical hoist to the waters edge ready for her re-christening and launching party. She had been re-registered as *Bluebird of Chelsea.*

Bluebird of Chelsea *on trials in 1986*

105

Martin Summers' daughter Tara with her friend Missy on
Bluebird of Chelsea *approaching Westminster Bridge*

ACT SIX

The Dream Fulfilled

". . . Here is the Happiness of the Blue Sky, of the Forest, of Sunny Hours and of Spring who is bright emerald. And then, when evening comes, here is the Happiness of Sunsets, who is grander than all the kings in the world, and who is followed by the Happiness of seeing the Stars Rise, who is gilded like a god of old . . ."

Maeterlinck,   *The Blue Bird*

To celebrate the restoration of Bluebird II
Martin Summers
invites you to attend her re-christening as

BLUEBIRD OF CHELSEA
by
Lady Summers
at
Salterns Marina, Poole
on
Saturday April 19th '86 at 1.00 p.m.

R.S.V.P.
Glebe Place Yacht Club
90 Oakley Street
London SW3   Lunch

The invitation to the launch party for **Bluebird of Chelsea**

As *Bluebird* was being rebuilt, the weeks and months, it seemed, went by far too slowly. I watched other owners enjoying their boats at Cadogan Pier and could hardly wait for *Bluebird* to take her place there. Then we reached the point when a date could be made for her launching and invitations were sent out including all who had been concerned with her rebuilding. With their respective partners, there would be more than one-hundred guests, including a coach-load brought down from London to Poole for the day.

Bluebird was lowered into the water at Poole Harbour Yacht Club and dressed overall. Though some of her fittings and deck furniture had not yet been completed, her freshly painted hull and brightwork were gleaming in the sun and she looked every inch a magnificent thorough-bred. The weather was kind, the guests lined the quayside dressed in blazers, straw hats and even period costumes. They cheered wildly when, on the stroke of one, my mother stepped forward from the family group of Tara, Scott and myself to break the traditional bottle of champagne across *Bluebird*'s bows and she re-named her *Bluebird of Chelsea*. It was a happy day for all of us and I was delighted to see how much the restoration of this famous wooden ship had meant to all the craftsmen who had shared in it. Everyone took great pride in a job well done.

There was still much to be completed and *Bluebird* stayed at Poole for over a week while she was fitted out for the sea voyage to her home on London's river. Throughout the restoration I had spoken with people about

Gina Campbell together with Martin Summers at **Bluebird of Chelsea**'s launching

109

the range and capability of ships of similar size and discovered that, although *Bluebird* had been built principally as an estuary cruiser, she had far greater potential than this. I began to speculate on what she might do and resolved to exploit her potential to the full. After all, Malcolm Campbell had used her competitively and after her thorough restoration we could be sure that she was totally seaworthy and unlikely to present us with unforeseen problems.

Under Scott's expert guidance her trials went well and after two days we set off on her maiden voyage to London. *Bluebird* immediately impressed us with the way she enjoyed the open sea. Her bilge keels stabilised her and she didn't roll as much as we had feared. The weather was fine, the ship was passing through familiar waters and we all felt thoroughly exhilarated. We spent a night in Ramsgate and left before dawn to catch a favourable tide on the Thames. Gina Campbell, Sir Malcolm Campbell's grand-daughter and now the holder of the ladies' water speed record, who had attended the launch party, made a rendezvous with us and on the dot of 12.15, exactly on schedule, she roared past us under Tower Bridge in *Agfa Bluebird* at an impressive 80 knots. Quite a sight!

Bluebird of Chelsea with Agfa Bluebird *in Battersea Reach, summer 1986*

We stopped at Tower Pier to collect my mother Scott's mother and Tara, and then proceeded proudly through the heart of London and past the Houses of Parliament for the first of many times. I had never seen London from its ancient highway and I shall never forget it. I am still thrilled every time I admire this beautiful and historic city from the river. I have since enjoyed this experience at least once a week with friends on board for an evening excursion up-river to Richmond or down to Greenwich leaving on the ebb and gliding back

110

soundlessly on the incoming tide through flood-lit London. On these occasions our wonderful Brazilian cook Louisa prepares a meal for us which is then served with the grace of a byegone age by George, our delightful steward.

At 1 o'clock at the end of our voyage from Ramsgate we arrived at *Bluebird's* permanent home at Cadogan Pier where during the next two months she received her finishing touches. Tom Brown came to stay at my house and worked a twelve-hour day on the ship. As part of our familiarisation we endlessly practised the docking procedure, gradually becoming accustomed to *Bluebird's* idiosyncrasies and the sometimes tricky tides and winds on the Thames. Now it all seems straightforward, but in the early days we had some anxious moments.

Soon after the relaunch we met John Knight, the Hon. Archivist of the Association of Dunkirk Little Ships, who was delighted to enroll *Bluebird of Chelsea* as a member. I had not bought the boat principally because she was a Dunkirk Little Ship. The fact that she had been to Dunkirk was a bonus and I came to appreciate that I had in her a piece of British history which held special significance for many people. It was important to Scott, for example, because his father had been at Dunkirk and owning *Bluebird* gave me a greater understanding of what this event meant for British people. I shall never forget the first time I sang "For Those in Peril on the Sea" at my first meeting of the Association in the chapel on St. Katharine's Dock. Through the window I could see the collection of Little Ships outside on the water while their owners joined in the hymn and with them I felt strangely moved by it all.

For our first real voyage we decided to take *Bluebird* to Holland and enjoy the Dutch canals. On a windless evening at the beginning of August 1986 we left Cadogan Pier at 9 o'clock on the ebb tide and dined on deck around

The house flag of the Association of Dunkirk Little Ships flown by member ships at the masthead. In addition, when sailing in company or when moored in harbour, members are entitled to fly the plain cross of St. George at the jackstaff

111

Bluebird *with her sun canopy rigged off Muiden Castle, 1986*

midnight. None of us felt tired and we watched the dawn come up on the Thames estuary to the music of Pavarotti. We had rigged a canopy over the aft deck which would probably have blown away had the sea not been like a mill pond with only a light breeze. After that voyage we took it down. It had proved useful on sunny days but in the end we came to feel that it was unsightly.

Exactly twenty-four hours after leaving Cadogan Pier we entered Ijmuiden Harbour in Holland where we began three happy weeks exploring the beautiful Dutch canals and the inland sea of the Isselmeer. *Bluebird* behaved admirably crossing the North Sea. Then, as ever since, she gave us great confidence and proved a fine sea-going ship. Even when she rolls she goes just so far and then stiffens and checks herself.

On our return journey we called at Dunkirk where *Bluebird*, proudly wearing her Dunkirk Little Ship flag, was instantly recognised as one of that historic flotilla of ships. Our return journey was delayed by three days by the tail-end of Hurricane Charlie which would have made the channel crossing dangerous.

Bluebird had proved herself to be such an ideal river and canal boat that in the summer of 1987 we chose to explore the French waterways. We crossed the channel without mishap and entered the French canal system at Calais. From there we entered the canal du Nord and along the river l'Oise to where it joins the Seine, then up the Seine to the Yonne as far as Auxerre. I can think of few experiences more pleasant than cruising through that

112

countryside, stopping here and there in sleepy little villages and mooring alongside the many excellent riverside restaurants. France offers almost limitless opportunities for canal and river cruising. From the north one can begin, as we did, from Calais and join the l'Oise or come up the Seine to Paris. From there the river Marne goes eastward to the Rhine or the Yonne takes you south to the Burgundy country and down the River Rhone as far as Marseille. On the west coast of France there is an extensive network of canals and rivers joining the Nore, or further south from Bordeaux one can enter the Dordogne or the Garonne which leads south-east to Toulouse and the canal du Midi all the way to the Mediterranean. *Bluebird* had of course crossed France before we found her, but we have not yet taken her back since her restoration.

Sunset at Villeneuve-sur-Yonne, summer 1987

In the summer of 1988 we felt drawn to the romantic western isles of Scotland, though one forgets that this is in fact further than the south of France. But our own British Isles offer some of the finest cruising grounds by sea, river and canal of any country in the world - if only the weather decides to be kind. Scott and Graham took *Bluebird* north along the east coast of England and made good time until the gearbox of the port engine blew up just short of Inverness. Fortunately the problem was quickly solved by the local marine agents, whose name, by strange coincidence was *Bluebird Services*. I flew to Inverness to join the ship with some friends and Anne, then my fiancé and now my wife. I had so hoped for beautiful weather, but for the next ten days it rained incessantly and even Loch Ness was rough. But the beauty of Urquart Castle, the Highlands

113

Bluebird *with* Undine *on Loch Ness near Urquart Castle, 1988*

and the Caledonian Canal itself made up for the bad weather. We did enjoy ourselves, although Anne ventured to ask wistfully about the possibility of having *Bluebird* in Positano one year. It has been a recurring thread through *Bluebird's* story that she has generally been loved by the owner more than by his partner. Happily I can say that Anne has come to enjoy *Bluebird* more and more and Scott's fiancé Gaynor loves to be on board.

We also cruised that year in convoy with Nick and Lucy Morris in their beautiful 68' ex-steam yacht *Undine of Solent*, built by Camper & Nicholson in 1895. Cruising in company the two ships received much admiration. We left Oban and spent two days in Loch Sunnart by the superb Glenborrodale Hotel. Our plan was to visit my friend Keith Schellenberg who owns the island of Eigg but on the way we encountered the roughest conditions yet. We were certainly extremely nervous but *Bluebird* almost seemed to relish the battle, for battle it was. But eventually we rounded Ardnamurchan Point and with much relief moored in the somewhat exposed Eigg Harbour. Keith met us in his delightful 1928 Rolls-Royce shooting brake and immediately challenged us, of all things, to a game of cricket. Despite the wind and rain and the odd stray sheep I am pleased to say that we achieved a narrow victory. That night after a superb dinner we were again victorious in a four-hour game of 'Campaign', much to the disgust of the highly competitive home team.

We stayed on Eigg for four happy days until the gale-force winds abated and I then had to return to London. From the safety of my home I would telephone Scott who

114

was bringing *Bluebird* back and monitor his progress south. Day by day he regaled me with hair-raising stories of heavy seas, but only on one occasion, near Aberdeen were they forced to seek shelter in Peterhead   Eventually the day came when I went down to meet a tired but happy crew at Cadogan Pier.

Also in 1988 *Bluebird* went to the Wooden Boat Show at Greenwich with her crew dressed by courtesy of Berman & Nathan's Costumiers.   The U-boat Commander's jacket and the German Officer's coat proved an unwise choice when we were visited by the First Sea-Lord, the Minister of Defence and the Captain of the Ark Royal but they invited us aboard their ship where the bemused sailors instinctively saluted our uniforms.

In 1989 we visited the champagne country.   We crossed to Le Havre and up the Seine to Paris.   From there we went down the River Marne towards Epernay where Anne and I joined Scott, Graham and Gaynor at Ferté-sus-Jouarre.   It was there, during eight days of sight-seeing on bicycles, that I found the family name on a tombstone on one of the vast World War cemeteries.   It made me shudder to see the evidence of thousands of young lives struck down in a gigantic waste of life.

On the way back we almost sailed into a trap.   We mentioned to a lock-keeper our intention to go on for a couple of days and then return.   He pointed out that a tunnel just round the corner on our route to Paris would be closed for six months.   Had we not mentioned it, our only alternative route to Calais would have included one-hundred-and-seventy locks and taken us three weeks!

Home again, *Bluebird* went to Henley and won the Thames Heritage Cup and the Denis Osland Trophy.   She was the first boat over

Bluebird at Henley where she won the Thames Heritage Cup in 1989

25' ever to have won a prize normally reserved for skiffs and the like and the first ADLS ship to have been so honoured.

1990 was to be the year devoted to the 50th anniversary return to Dunkirk by all those Little Ships who could make it. Seventy-three succeeded with great credit to the Association and their owners because for many of them it required a supreme effort. Some had worked on their boats for years to make this crossing and many of them knew that once it was over they would not be able to afford to keep them. For old wooden boats are expensive to maintain. In January *Bluebird* went to Tough's Boat Yard of Teddington to prepare for the jubilee return and she came back looking magnificent. We were determined to bring her even closer to her original appearance. Now I believe *Bluebird* is exactly how we want her to be.

Prince Philip reviewing the Little Ships of Dunkirk assembled in Dunkirk Harbour together with David Rolt (Commodore) and Raymond Baxter (Hon. Admiral of the Association of Dunkirk Little Ships)

We came to Dover rather later than most boats and found Dover Harbour ablaze with bunting. Owners were still working on their boats when Prince Philip arrived to inspect the fleet. Such was his interest in the Little Ships and the bemedalled veterans who had secured berths in them, we all felt that he would have been happy to come with us. The weather forecast was promising: with wind speeds of force 3 and decreasing so that we could expect calm seas and a good crossing. Thousands of people lined the harbour to watch us go. At high tide the lock opened and the seventy-six Little Ships spilt out to get into their twin-column, four-a-breast formation. But almost immediately they

116

hit the roughest patch of water that many of them had ever experienced. Boats wallowed in the swell and we wondered how we could endure an estimated nine hours of this - (unaware that it was going to take fourteen hours!) The wind blew at force 6 during the crossing and, just like during

Bluebird of Chelsea *ploughing into the heavy swell on leaving Dover Harbour, 24th May 1990*

those fateful days fifty years ago, many of the Little Ships broke down. This tested the resourcefulness of their crews, many of whom succeeded in repairing their engines without leaving the fleet and simply reported their progress by VHF radio to David Rolt, the Commodore. He showed amazing calm and resourcefulness throughout the voyage occasionally asking our escorts, HMS *Alacrity,* HMS *Ledbury,* RNXSV *Example* and the support ship *Rose Harty* to come to the aid of ships who lost all their engine power. In the end, three had to turn back. Behind the Commodore and the Hon. Admiral followed a mile-long flotilla of Little Ships, with the smallest in front and the largest at the rear, proceeding at a speed of four-and-a-half knots through one of the world's busiest stretches of water. We crossed the separation zone with super-tankers and cargo-ships passing across our bows first from the port side and later from starboard. From time to time the whole fleet was ordered to change direction so as to avoid one of them. RNXSV *Example* was just like a mother duck taking her ducklings across a motorway.

After six hours we were still within sight of Dover and the French coast was just a blur on the horizon. Then suddenly a Spitfire came over low, performed a barrel-roll

117

Bluebird *passing the war-damaged mole at the entrance of Dunkirk Harbour*

The 50th anniversary plaque presented to each Little Ship by the Mayor of Dunkirk

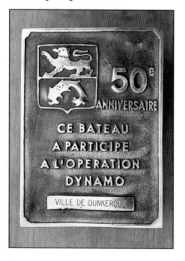

followed by a loop, dipped its wings in salute and returned to England. It was a moving sight and as we reached the French coast near Calais, turning east along the buoyed channel towards Dunkirk, our thoughts turned to the brave crews who arrived here fifty years ago. German guns were trained on them along the coast between Calais and Dunkirk and Stuka dive-bombers dropped their bombs and strafed them with machine-gun fire. All we had to contend with was the freshening breeze and the tide gradually turning against us so that our progress became even slower and we reached Dunkirk in the falling light. The derelict mole at the entrance of Dunkirk Harbour made it easy to imagine the scene as the Little Ships found it in 1940. Our berths were in the Bassin du Commerce but we first had to pass through a lock - all seventy-three of us - and then find our reserved mooring places. It all required a great deal of patience and boat-handling skill but the dock-masters of the ADLS did a magnificent job in getting us there.

The next evening the Mayor of Dunkirk presented each Little Ship with a solid brass anniversary plaque. There were speeches designed to reinforce Anglo-French friendship and the British Commercial Attaché provided instantaneous translations.

On Sunday *Bluebird,* together with her sister ships, slipped her moorings at noon, went out through the lock and joined a large circle of Little Ships for the service of commemoration off La Panne. 7,000 Dunkirk veterans lined the beach and on the seaward side the Navy was anchored to guard the fleet. A naval helicopter lowered a winchman to lay a wreath in the water, a Spitfire, a

118

Hurricane and a Lancaster bomber made three passes overhead and the Red Arrows provided a fly-past. The highlight of our journey and the reason for our return was over.

Cheering crowds welcoming home Bluebird of Chelsea *and the whole fleet of Little Ships from their 50th anniversary pilgrimage to Dunkirk*

Next day we left Dunkirk Harbour at dawn. The weather was dull as we took our formation and the wind had dropped. By 9 a.m. the sun had appeared and our members' spirits had risen. Our return to Ramsgate was only marred by the occasional intrusion of spectator boats who infiltrated the strict formation of the Little Ships. At Ramsgate 10,000 people lined every vantage point. Bands were playing, the spectators cheered and some Dunkirk veterans carrying Royal British Legion flags could be seen in tears. It was a great home-coming for the Little Ships.

Now *Bluebird*, almost sixty years old, is ready for the future. She will always be a proud member of the Association of Dunkirk Little Ships, and hopefully will set an example of faithful restoration and incessant preservation to keep her looking just as good on the 100th anniversary of 'Operation Dynamo'; for boats properly cared for can live longer than people.

I hope to enjoy her to the end of my days and to see a little more of the rivers and waterways of Europe every year while letting her play her part in the annual round of life on the Thames. We would like to go back to the West Country one day soon, where as *Blue Bird* and *Bluefinch* she spent so much of her time, and explore the beautiful River Dart. We want to go further up the Thames beyond Reading and perhaps as far as Oxford. Another voyage to the Caledonian

119

Martin and Scott celebrating with a commemorative bottle of Campbeltown whisky engraved: **Operation Dynamo, 1940 - 1990**

Canal is planned and we shall certainly go back to the canals of Holland and France. I should love to take *Bluebird* to the Mediterranean but the journey takes twenty-two days each way, which means that I could not have her on the Thames for one whole English summer and I can hardly bear the thought. *Bluebird* is such an important part of our lives although she at times throws tantrums and I believe she has a soul. When she takes the bit between her teeth and shows the wilful character I have come to respect and love, I know she is enjoying the life she is leading now and fulfilling the destiny for which she was created. I think that Sir Malcolm Campbell also would approve.

Bluebird*'s crew in 1990 left to right:*
Tone, Tara, Alexander, Scott , Martin, Celia, Gaynor, Paula

Next row: Graham, George, Anne, Nastasya, and Louisa

120

APPENDIX   Record of Fittings

Here is a complete list of the items ordered and received by Thornycroft's between 28th May and 21st August 1931 for use on *Blue Bird*, together with suppliers and costs. They are items which were not carried as yard stock or in general stores, and therefore had to be bought in. Prices are shown in the pre-decimalisation monetary system of pounds, shillings and pence. There were 20 shillings (expressed as 20/-) to the pound (£) and 12 pence (expressed as 12d) to the shilling. Hence, for example, two shillings and ten pence was written as 2/10, and two pounds ten shillings (now £2.50) as £2/10/-.

To put costs into perspective, we can compare them with some wages and the prices of a few commodities today. The average weekly wage for a man in the year *Blue Bird* was built was around £3 and was on a slight downward trend from that of the 1920s. The weekly wages of women workers averaged £1/19/6 (£1.97). Even so, a good experienced skilled worker might attain £5, and his unskilled counterpart £4. Men retiring could look forward to a weekly state pension of 10/- (50p).

A small suburban, semi-detached, two-bedroomed house cost £250-£300; for twice that amount one could buy a large, three-bedroom house in a nice residential area. And the little Austin 12 family saloon car would have cost £235; nearly as much as the smaller house. *Blue Bird*, then, would have cost Malcolm Campbell at least the equivalent of two fair-sized family homes plus a motor car.

If Thornycroft's men enjoyed a pint after their hard work on *Blue Bird*, they would have paid the equivalent of $2^{1/2}$p. If their tipple was something stronger, 13/- (65p) bought them a bottle of whisky but made a big hole in their weekly wage.

And when they put on the kitchen table what was left on a Friday night, no doubt their wives grumbled about the price of groceries. Sugar was now tuppence three farthings (1p) a pound, bread cost 9d (4p) a loaf, eggs were 1/6 ($7^{1/2}$p) a dozen, tea had rocketed to almost 2/6 (12p) a pound. If they expected jam a one pound pot would set back the housekeeping budget by 1/- (5p).

28th May 1931
12' centreboard sailing dinghy complete as inspected by Messrs. Thornycroft (J. King & Co. Ltd.: £38)
29th May 1931
Galv. $5/8$" bolts and nuts, standard square heads, all lengths overall complete with washers 1-14$^{1/2}$": 1-18": 1-14$^{3/4}$": 1-19": 1-16": 1-20$^{1/2}$": 1-17": 1-21": 1-18": 1-22$^{1/2}$": 1-20$^{1/4}$": 1-23$^{1/2}$": 1-22": 1-26": 1-24": 1-28$^{1/2}$": 2-26": 1-31" (A.T. Chamberlain: £1/14/6)
1 cast iron keel off wood pattern (Kingston Foundries: £13/14/9)
10th June 1931
6 doz. 2" x $5/16$" galv. coach screws, sq. head (G. Hatch: 5/- the lot)
1 galv. steel bulkhead to BP 21384 (J. Taylor Ltd.: £17/10)
1 galv. steel anchor davit to BP 20611 (J. Taylor Ltd.: £4/5/6)
18 No 4 Fly 307 SL portlights (Simpson Lawrence: £1/17/3 each)
loose outside rings (Simpson Lawrence)
Alterations to shaft bracket pattern (T. Valley Pattern Works: £1/18/-)
2 $3/4$" gas gunmetal three way lock with handles (Lamberts Ltd.: 15/3)
3 Blakes Baby WC complete with covers to seat (Blake & Co.: 9/- each)
1 off 6' x 2' x 1'6" G cot frame and canvas (Chamberlain : £1/3/6)
2 off 4" copper cowl vents complete with coaming cap (Chamberlain)
1 boathook GM head (A.T. Chamberlain & Co.: 17/9)
1 galv. stock anchor (A.T. Chamberlain & Co: £1/17/6)
1 hollow kedge anchor (A.T. Chamberlain & Co.: £1/-/-)

5 off 4" mushroom ventilators (J.D. Lang & Co: 17/6 each)
1 set copper navigating lamps (J.D. Lang & Co.)
5 off PSMS & R. Baston burners (J.D. Lang & Co.)
1 paraffin cooker No 021 (Taylor Paraffin Ltd: £8/17/6)
1 paraffin cooker No 023 (Taylor Paraffin Ltd.: £7/-/-)
3$^{1/2}$' single ash block cathook and becket (Dyne & Evans: £11/10)
11th June 1931
1 galv. iron tabernacle to BP 20358 (J. Taylor Ltd.: £1/15/6)
1 Record vice with 4" jaws (Nurse: 18/8)
2 prs. GM fairleads 12" (Greenway & Clive: 7/3 each)
1 galv. windlass (Greenway & Clive: £3/17/6)
25 fathoms galv. short link chain (Greenway: £2/18/11)
12th June 1931
100 gall. fuel tank to SK914 (Braby: £7/15/-)
2 x 100 gall. fuel tanks comp. to B print (Richards: £13/19/6)
15th June 1931
2 off 8" x $7/8$" x $3/16$" brass skylight quadrants (Greenway: 5/3)
2 off 3" brass sliding door locks 3" x$1/2$" (Greenway: 8/3 each)
2 off 4" x 2" brass flush sliding door handles (Greenway: 1/6 each)
8 brass sash rollers 2" x $7/8$" (Greenway: 1/- each)
2 prs. spec casement fasteners (open out) (Greenway: 6/9 each)
1 r.h. W.C. lock with striking plate (Greenway: 7/-)
8 sets oval knobs & rim furn. shallow (Greenway: 6/- each)

121

20 spring drawer handles $3^{1/2}$" x 2" (Greenway: 1/4 each)
18 off 2" sill locks (Greenway: 1/9 each)
2 left hand rim locks 4" x 3" box plate (Greenway: 8/- each)
5 left hand wardrobe locks (Greenway: 5/- each)
8 sets oval knob & knob ward. furn. (Greenway: 3/9 each)
2 off 3" spring drawer handles (Greenway: 1/3 each)
4 off $3^{1/2}$" x $^{7/16}$" brass table screws (Greenway: 3/6)
2" brass cill lock (Greenway: 1/9)
$1^{1/2}$" brass cill lock (Greenway: 1/9)
1" brass screw knob (Greenway: 10/-)
2 left hand W.C. locks (Greenway: 7/- each)
3 right hand wardrobe locks (Greenway: 5/- each)
1 right hand brass rim lock (Greenway: 8/-)
1 doz $2^{1/4}$" wardrobe hooks (Greenway: 3/8 per dozen)
12 off $2^{1/2}$" x $1^{1/2}$" spring drawer handles (Greenway: 1/- each)
1 left hand rim lock with striking plate (Greenway: 8/-)
1 pair cross garnets (Greenway: £1/3/-)
2 off 2" brass padlocks (Greenway: 6/9 each)
2 off 4" x 2" flush sliding door handles to be chromium plated (Greenway: 2/3)
2 castings Ad. GM pattern 2184 (Kingston Foundries: 5/11)
4 castings (Kingston Foundries: 2/10)
2 castings (Kingston Foundries: £7/5/-)

16th June 1931
1 casting off pattern 1510 rope wheel (Kingston Foundries)
2 galv. iron knees template 1, 2 galv. iron knees template 2, 2 galv. iron knees template 3, 2 galv. iron knees template 4 (J. Taylor Ltd.: £3/2/6)
1 galv. iron stemband per template (Chamberlain : £2/17/6)
3" plunger pump discharge under (Chamberlain: £3.15/-)
$^{3/4}$" seacock (Blake & Sons: 10/-)
1 fig. H2794 pol shower (Shanks & Co. Ltd.: 12/-)
1 fig. H4029 stopcock (Shanks & Co. Ltd.: 8/-)
2 off $^{1/2}$" brass pillar cocks (Shanks & Co.: 7/- each)
$^{3/4}$" waste union complete (Lamberts Ltd.: 1/6)
2 off $1^{1/2}$" galv. fullway gate valves (Lamberts Ltd.: 18/6)
1 $^{1/2}$ galv. fourway piece (Lamberts Ltd.: 10/-)
6 off $1^{1/2}$" brass nipples (Lamberts Ltd: 4/-)
1 complete set G.I. rudder gear as per blue print (Taylor : £5/10)

18th June 1931
4 pieces $17^{1/2}$" x $9^{3/8}$" x $^{1/4}$" plate glass (Cliffords Ltd.: 4/5)
2 castings Ad. GM patt. 1634 t.p. caps (Kingston Foundries: 6/6)
2 off 4" torpedo ventilators GM (Thorn & Hoddle)
1 size E (No. 1) combined compressor and chain pipe (Pascal Atkey & Son £2/15/-)
GM drum plate spindle to take 24" wheel (Chamberlain: 28/6)
2 no. O C semi rotary pump (Chamberlain: £2/12/6)
3 piece mirror plate 18" x 5" x $^{3/4}$" (Cliffords Ltd.: 19/9)
2 spring frame mattresses 6' x 2' (Haskins & Sewell: £1/2/6 each)
1 spring frame mattress template A (Haskins & Sewell: £1/2/6)
1 spring frame mattress template B (Haskins & Sewell: £1/2/6)

50 gall. fresh water tank as per SK915 (Braby)
1 comp. set ironwork as per B.P. 322 (J. Taylor Ltd.)
30ft. of No. 51 rubber covered cable (J. Taylor Ltd.)
2 Rawlings windows as per sketch (Rawlings Manufacturing Co.: £2/4/6 each)
Finsbury No. 3 geyser (oil) (Winterflood Geyser Co.: £10/10/-)
Fig 387 searchlight, 2 off bulb (Simpson Lawrence: £8/2/-)
Fig 291: $3^{1/2}$" dial clock (Simpson Lawrence: £2/13/-)
Fig 292: $3^{1/2}$" aneroid (Simpson Lawrence: £1/14/6)
1 set code flags 24 x 18 (Simpson Lawrence: £2/14/-)
Lavatory basin Fig 59 waste 1 cold tap, china plug for hot tap hole and 1 pr. white enamel brackets (Simpson Lawrence: £3/10/-)
$^{1/2}$ kw shunt wound dynamo st. set, battery charging 25/35 volts water cooled silencer, shunt regulators (Stuart Turner: £49/10/-)
1 model 75 Kelvinator comp. with dry system cooling unit, motor suitable for 24 volts (Kelvinator: £52/15/-)
1 comp. set galv. iron stanchions, rail, wire guards etc. BP 21394 (J. Taylor Ltd.: £61/3/-)

23rd June 1931
2 Fig 624 folding lavatories with mirror on top plate (Simpson Lawrence: £6/13/-)
12 castings Towing post whelps (Kingston Foundries: 7/6)
2 Fig. 222A 12" gas cylinder cock union to take $^{1/2}$" o.d. copper pipe (Bells Asbestos Co.: 15/-)
Engrave "Fresh Water" on filler cap (Reliance Eng. Co.: 2/-)

24th June 1931
2 off $3^{1/2}$" double ash blocks with fixed eye and becket (eye to take $^{3/4}$" diam. pin) (Dyne & Evans Ltd.)
2 off $3^{1/2}$" double ash blocks with fast hooks (Dyne & Evans Ltd.)

25th June 1931
18ft. No. 59 rubber covered cable (Vanderwells: at 1/1 per foot)
10 c.v. fittings, metal part chromium plated with glasses (Vanderwells: 20/8)
2 CK inspection lamps w. 12' of cable (Vanderwells: 12/6 each)
2 castings patt 1984 stern tube slipper (Kingston Foundries: £3/6/11)
Chr. plate 8 brass rods (at 2/6), 3 prs. hinges (at 1/4 per pair),1 hasp (2/3), 66 screws (at 5/- per gross), 1 staple (2/3), 138 mac screws & nuts, 3" cleat (1/2), 1 lamp socket, (2/3), 1 gross $^{5/8}$" x 6 screws (5/-), 2 gross screw eyes (at 4/- per gross), 13 pairs stair treads (at 2/- per foot), $2^{1/2}$" deck fillers (at 2/6 each), 3 towing post pins (at 9d each), 2" socket (2/2), towing post cap, 1 ensign socket (2/2), 1 set of 5 copper lamps (£4/10/-), 17 portlights and flanges (18/6 each), 2 mushroom vents (9/- each), 4 ladder sockets (10d each) 216 1 x 12 screws (at 5/- per gross) (J. Griffiths)
Brass curtain rods 18" long , 18 pairs curtain rod ends , 18 pairs curtains in blue casement cloth as per sample colour 24" deep width to suit 18" rods, 18 pairs tie up hooks (Chamberlain: £8/6/9)
2 Hobson guages, handed, each with 30' pipeline for tanks BP 21382 (William Hobson Ltd.: £7/10/-)
2" x $^{1/2}$" brass plate off each: freshwater suction, tray suction, discharge overboard, shower bath, suction from seacock, freshwater to geyser (Reliance Engraving Co.)

122

1 pair $2^{1/4}$" diam. davits with all fittings to BP 21391 (Blake: £12/12/6)

1 Fig. 309 letter C 10" x 3" oblong deck lights (Simpson L.: 7/4 each)

22 SBC 25v 20w bulbs (Siemens Brothers Electric Co.: 3/- each)

Brass lamp fork, chromium plated (£1/17/6), 1 brass hatch stanchion socket & hook etc. (£2/9/6), 4 x 6" gm shroud plates (2/9 each), $4^{5/16}$" Reiach rigging screws at 10/6 each (Chamberlain)

1 piece blue lino 36'x6' (£3/18/-), 1 piece black & white lino 14' x 6' (£1/19/-) (T. Moggridge)

1" gas full-way gate valve (9/-), $1^{1/2}$" gas full-way gate valve (18/6) (Lamberts Ltd.)

27th June 1931

5" card compass 'Dead beat' type (Reynolds, Son, Dobbie & Clyde)

Chromium plate: 7 roof lamp fittings (at 2/-), 3 doz. screws (at 1/3), portlight flange (J. Griffiths)

15 gallon fuel tank with all fittings to BP 21398. Filler to be chrom. plated (D. J. Hawkins: £3/17/-)

29th June 1931

12v standard model chrom. plated horn (£8/16/-) Cicca electric horn (S. Smith & Sons.)

Fit 1 Simm's gauge to 15 gall. tank (D.J. Hawkins: £1/10/-)

2 pieces $^{1/4}$" plate glass temp A, 1 piece temp B, one piece temp C, 2 pieces temp D, one edge ground, 2 pieces temp E one edge ground and notches and 2 pieces temp F (Cliffords Ltd.: £4/13/10)

30th June 1931

20 fathoms $^{5/16}$" galvanised short link chain suitable for winch to windlass (G. Ure & Co.)

Adapt one acetylene searchlight to electric chrom. plate and supply bulb (Thorn & Hoddle)

Chromium plate 3" cleat & frame (J. Griffiths)

1 galvanised iron ladder 6' x 12" (Chamberlain)

2 pcs. copper stove pipe 6'6" x 4" diameter (Chamberlain: (£1/5/9 each)

1st July 1931

1 No. 4 Fig 307 sl portlights with outside ring (Simpson Lawrence 37/3)

1 CD fitting with clear glass (Vanderwells: £1/0/8)

4 x $1^{1/2}$" tank unions with nut and lines (Lamberts Ltd.: 19/6 each)

2nd July 1931

Chromium plate: 1 hatch strap (4/6), 3 mushroom vents (9/- each), 2 ladder hooks (1/2 each), 4 fairleads (8/6 each) and 12 whelps (1/- each) (J. Griffiths)

10 Bakelite switch plates & switches (G. Johnson: 1/9 each)

4 fathoms 2" circ. cable laid white cotton rope (H. Bannister: 8/2)

Engrave caps with words "Fresh Water" (Reliance Eng. Co.: 2/-)

1 comp. set galvanised ironwork BP 21399 (Tom Taylor: £3/14/-)

3rd July 1931

$1^{1/2}$" yard red ensign, $1^{1/2}$ yard blue ensign (Adam & Lane & Neeve)

Chromium plate: 1 pump on top only (5/6), 1 plate, (2/6) 7 machine screws (7d each), 2 towing post caps (4/- each), 1 deck filler (2/6) (J. Griffiths)

7th July 1931

Chromium plate: 2" filler (2/6), $3^{1/2}$" x $^{3/16}$" split pins, 3 pins, 4 pieces $^{3/16}$" x $^{1/16}$" brass strip (J. Griffiths)

1 piece of white hide 2'6" x 1'6" (Dawson & Co.)

1" waste union complete (Lamberts Ltd.: 2/9)

Upholster wood frames for cushions with springs covered in blue Atho leather colour No. 032. Upholster wood frame backs stuffed kapok in blue Atho leather colour No. 032. (8 cushions and backs, 2 spare cushions). (Chamberlain: £34/5/10)

Chromium plate, 1 whelp, 1 search light & 2 filler caps (J. Griffiths: £3/17/6)

1 single pole change -over switch $4^{1/2}$" x 2" GEC Company)

8th July 1931

1 brass curtain rod 7'9" x $^{1/2}$" diam. with two end fittings, 1 blue casement cloth 5'10" deep to match curtains (£2/3/6) (Chamberlain)

Engrave word "petrol" on 2 filler caps (Reliance Eng. Co.: 1/9 each)

1 roller and plate for No. 2 Bruce capstan (Pascal Atkey: 10/-)

9th July 1931

Chromium plate 1 socket & 8 mac screws (J. Griffiths)

1 No. O.C. semi-rotary pump (Chamberlain: £2/12/6)

15th July 1931

1 left hand brass rimlock 5 x 3 upright with striking plate (Greenway & Clive: 8/-)

1 piece of glass $12^{3/16}$" x $7^{5/8}$" (Cliffords Ltd.: 6d)

1 piece copper stove pipe (12/6) 24" sea anchor (15/-) (Chamberlain)

Engrave on filler cap "petrol" (Reliance Eng. Co.: 1/9)

Launder 5 roller and 2 hand towels (Hampton Laundry)

Chromium plate: 1 piece brass tube 1" x $^{5/8}$" (5d), $^{1/2}$" washer (2d), portlight flange (18/6), 1 mushroom vent (9/-), 4 pieces of tread (8/6), 4 cabin hooks (8/-), 2 dozen screws (10d), (J. Griffiths)

mirror 12" or 14" long $9^{1/2}$" wide with $^{3/4}$" bevel and hole in each corner (Cliffords Ltd.)

1 lavatory basin top as supplied to order marked hot but for $^{3/4}$" gas (Simpson Lawrence)

2 brass stop valves fig. 107 for $^{3/4}$" copper pipe (Lamberts Ltd.: 11/-)

4 brass stop end stanchions (A.T. Chamberlain: 5/6 each)

3 brass through stanchions for $1^{1/8}$" tube , $2^{1/4}$" from base to centre of eye (A.T. Chamberlain: 5/6 each)

85lb galv. stock anchor with gravity band (Chamberlain: £2/2/6)

2 wicker chairs No. 126 w. rubber shoes (W. J. Ellmore & Co.: £1/14/6 each)

1 mattress in tick to template (A.T. Chamberlain: £1/5/-)

3 off 6" clear glass decklights chrom. plated (A.T. Chamberlain: 16/6)

1 anchor and line suitable for launch (J. King & Co.: 15/-)

Round off 5 lamp shades and polish end (Cliffords Ltd.: 2/6)

16th July 1931

1 x 6 gall. f.w. tank as per sketch (Thorn & Hoddle: 15/6)

1 Bakelite switch and plate (G. Johnston: 1/9)

2 inverted flambeau glasses (G.Johnston: 2/6)

2 pieces rubber (weathering) for $^{1/4}$" glass each 27" long (Rawlings Manufacturing Co.: 2/4)

Fig 70 water filter comp. (Simpson Lawrence : £2/2/-)

Brass plate 1' x $^{1/2}$" engraved "earthing wire" (1/9) and Brass plate 1' x $^{1/2}$" engraved "aerial to earth" (1/9) (Reliance Engraving Co.)

1 single pole change -over switch $4^{1/2}$" x 2 (G.E.C.: 2/-)

123

6 batten holders SBC (G.E.C.: 5/6)

1 switch and fuse 5 amp (G.E.C.: 5/6)

6 x 25v, 25w SBC bulbs (G.E.C.: 3/-)

1 x 5 amp crocus wood socket (G.E.C.: 2/3)

20th July 1931

Chr. plate 2 pieces 6' x 1" brass strip (J. Griffiths & Son.: 9d each)

21st July 1931

1 burgee 12 x 18 with *Blue Bird* painted on (A.T. Chamberlain 6/9d): Alter curtains as follows: All bobbles to be removed and sides to be piped. Bottoms to be hemmed and shot-loaded. Lengths to be altered (A.T. Chamberlain: £2/12/-)

1 gravity band for 75lb anchor (A.T. Chamberlain)

2 pieces 8'6" long brass tube $1^{1/8}$" for stanchions (Chamberlain: 18/6)

6 red Verey cartridges (6/6), (Chamberlain)

2 red hurricane lamps (A.T. Chamberlain: 5/6 each)

Chromium plate: 8 Ad. GM stanchions (2/6 each), 46 off $1^{1/4}$" x $^{1/4}$" mac screws (3/10), 20 nuts (5/-), 20 washers (2/6), 12 off $1^{3/4}$" x 10 screws (6d) (J. Griffiths)

1 centre curtain rod fitting (through) for $^{3/4}$" rod to hinge or clip (1/-), 2 pairs end fittings (1/9), 3 curtain rods $^{3/8}$" x 2' (2/-) (Chamberlain)

22nd July 1931

Chr. plate 2 brass tubes (J. Griffiths)

23rd July 1931

Chromium plate: 2 off 8'3" lengths $1^{1/8}$" brass tube, 24 screws, 4 hinged buttons (1/-), 3 x 10" pieces stair tread (at 1/9d each) (J. Griffiths & Son.)

27th July 1931

2 x 25v, 20w bulbs (small) (2/- each), $^{1/2}$ doz 25v, 20w bulbs (3/2 each) (Siemens Brothers Electric Company)

2 x 4" treble ash blocks with fast hooks and becket to take $1^{3/4}$" rope (18/9 each), and 2 x 4" double ash blocks with fixed eye to take $^{5/8}$" bolt (18/9 each) (Dyne & Evans)

40 fathoms 1" manilla (A.T. Chamberlain: 10/6)

2 gangway fenders (white canvas) about 10" diameter (Chamberlain: 10/6 each)

28th July 1931

Services of compass adjuster (Reynolds & Son, Dobbie & Clyde: £3/3/-)

1 30" RTYC Burgee (Adam, Lane & Neeve: 6/-)

1st August 1931

1 gooseneck to $^{1/2}$" patt. 1708 (Davey & Co.: 8/6)

1 galv. boom cup $^{1/2}$" (Davey & Co.)

7th August 1931

1 No. OC semi rotary pump (all brass) (A.T. Chamberlain: £2/12/6)

11th August 1931

1 combined chain pipe and compressor for $^{3/8}$" chain (Pascal, Atkey & Co.: £3/5/-)

1 galvanised iron windlass for $^{3/8}$" galv. short line chain shackled in 10 fathom lengths by cableshackles and large link each end (G. Ure & Co.: £4/12/6)

21st August 1931

Fit new winch and compressor to *Blue Bird* (Woolston Works: £1/10/-)

Picture Credits   a = above, b = below, (r) = right

124

INDEX

Index

Index

Index

H23 819 132 7

A CHARGE
IS MADE FOR
REMOVED OR
DAMAGED
LABELS.

ARRANGEMENT OF MOTOR YACHT

SCALE ½ INCH = 1 FOOT

FEET

METRES

THORNYCROFT

12 FT. MOTOR DINGHY

BOAT Nº 2246